MW00777176

Heavenly Sandpaper

A Caregiver's Journey Through a Stem Cell Transplant

Barbara Betts

CROSSBOOKS
PUBLISHING

CrossBooks™
A Division of LifeWay
1663 Liberty Drive
Bloomington, IN 47403
www.crossbooks.com
Phone: 1-866-879-0502

First published by CrossBooks 2/16/2010

ISBN: 978-1-6150-7141-8 (sc)

Library of Congress Control Number: 2010901763

Printed in the United States of America
Bloomington, Indiana

This book is printed on acid-free paper.

Unless otherwise noted, all Scripture references are taken from the New International Version (NIV): From the *Holy Bible, New International Version,* copyright © 1973, 1978, 1984 by International Bible Society.

Other versions include:

Scripture quotations marked (*The Message*) are taken from *The Message* by Eugene H. Peterson, copyright © 1993, 1994, 1995, 1996, 2000, 2001, 2003. Used by permission of NavPress Publishing Group. All rights reserved.

Scripture quotations marked (NLT) are taken from the *Holy Bible, New*

Living Translation, copyright © 1996. Used by permission of Tyndale House Publishers, Inc., Wheaton, IL 60189 USA. All rights reserved.

Scripture quotations marked (NASB) are taken from the *New American Standard Bible®*, Copyright ©1960, 1962, 1963, 1968, 1971, 1972, 1973, 1975, 1977, 1995 by the Lockman Foundation. Used by permission. (www.lockman.org)

Scripture quotations marked (NKJV) are from the New King James Version. Copyright © 1979, 1980, 1982, Thomas Nelson, Inc., Publishers.

Scripture quotations marked (TLB) are taken from The Living Bible, copyright ©1971. Used by permission of Tyndale House Publishers, Inc., Wheaton, IL 60189 USA. All rights reserved.

Scripture quotations marked HCSB® are taken from the *Holman Christian Standard Bible®*, copyright © 1999, 2000, 2001, 2002 by Holman Bible Publishers. Used by permission.

Scriptures marked (KJV) are from the King James Version of the Bible.

Scripture quotations marked (NCV) are from *The Holy Bible, New Century Version,* copyright © 1987, 1988, 1991 by W Publishing Group, Nashville, TN 37214. Used by permission.

To my husband, Bill.
As we live and grow together in Him,
I thank Him more and more
For all the ways you bless my life.
You meet each challenge with courageous fortitude and faith
You have loved me, and inspired me
In more ways than I can express as we journey
Toward our Promised Land

This book is also dedicated to all the caregivers
Who love and support their patients
To the wonderful staff at Vanderbilt University Medical Center, and
M.D. Anderson Cancer Center who have given my husband
The best medical care throughout our journey
Thank you!

Acknowledgments

I sensed God wanted me to write this book, but I was reluctant. Why? Because I've never done anything like this before, and I certainly do not consider myself a professional writer. I'm a wife, a mom, and a grandmother. I wrote newsletters to our family, church family, and friends to keep them informed of what was happening in our lives while Bill and I were miles away from our home and family, receiving his stem-cell transplant. I was told a caregiver needed to keep everyone updated on the progress of the patient. That's what I did.

The newsletters became a way for me to express what was happening in my life. I began to hear how people were sharing our newsletters and encouraging me to write a book about this journey. I laughed that thought off, "write a book, no way, not me!"

Over time, after more encouragement, I began to think maybe this is what I was to do. My husband and close friends kept saying, "You can do this." However, I kept coming up with many excuses why I couldn't. I don't have time, Lord. I have a full-time job, and we have just had our third grandbaby. I just started teaching a ladies Bible study class, and so on.

When the Lord has other plans, He will not give you peace until you say yes. I told the Lord, "I can't do this," as He reminded me of Philippians 4:13. "I can do everything through him who gives me strength." I told the Lord, "I'll do it, but You are going to have to show me how." That's how it started. I pushed past my insecurities and started writing; my pen just kept moving!

Seeing how God has worked through me to write this book is humbling. I want to say a special thanks to my husband, who believed that I could do this. His endless encouragement has been my greatest gift. Bill is the love of my life, my partner, and I am blessed beyond measure. He has shared my dreams and helped make them come true. What I have learned from him has given me the inspiration to write. His courageous preaching of the Word of God has influenced and continues to bless and profoundly affect my life. He is a daily help in my walk of faith and I could not do what I do without him.

I give praise to God and thanks to the many who have prayed for us through this journey. With your faithful, consistent prayers, you prayed us through many difficult moments. Those prayers and God's Word indeed renewed our strength. Because of your extraordinary involvement in our journey, you enabled me to want to share this story. Our love and blessings be upon you.

Table of Contents

Introduction

Have you ever been faced with an adversity that doesn't seem fair and you wonder why this is happening now when life has been going along so smoothly? Can anything good come from these sufferings and trials? Are your struggles causing you to doubt God's love for you and His purposes? Those questions seemed to peel back the layers of my heart as I dealt with my husband's cancer and the daily circumstances that surrounded our lives. Bill and I would live through one of the darkest times we had ever encountered in our thirty-eight years of marriage. This cancer had gotten out of control, and nothing was stopping it from destroying Bill's body. It appeared his life would be cut short and our dreams of growing old together in our retirement years might not happen. Losing the love of my life was not something I was prepared to deal with, nor could I ever imagine life without him. When a detour around the roadblock became an option, we took it. I became my husband's caregiver as we traveled down the road of a stem-cell transplant and the days of recovery that followed.

You will read about my heart-wrenching personal struggles. As a caregiver, I sometimes laughed, and sometimes cried, but I was determined not to be defeated. This journey took us miles away from our family and friends, but Bill and I felt the prayers and support of their love. The power of prayer was overwhelming! As life and death played out day and night, seven days a week, month after month, we saw God's faithfulness in every detail of this journey and I learned many things about trusting God. When you are in the midst of dealing with an adversity, it is easy to focus on it and forget that God wants us to see His fingerprints all over this experience. God had much to teach me about His faithfulness. I sometimes walked, other times I crawled, but God always sustained me.

I invite you to go with me on this journey. You will learn about a stem-cell transplant through the eyes of this caregiver as I share information about the process of a stem-cell transplant for it is becoming a treatment option for many diseases. Stem cell transplantation is a procedure where healthy, normal blood forming cells are infused into a person. Donor stem cells would graft into Bill's bone marrow which is the spongy tissue found inside the cavities of large bones replacing his diseased cells with new cells. If the transplant is successful, these new cells will begin to grow and produce normal cells that will eventually develop into mature healthy tissues giving new life and hopefully destroying any remaining cancer cells.

You will hear about the great strides that have been made in the donor process, the preparative regimen that is the countdown period before transplantation of stem cells, and then what it was like caring for the patient during the many months of recovery. You will learn about the difference between embryonic stem cells and adult stem-cells.

I will share those early years of Bill's cancer treatments before his stem cell transplant. You will see my raw emotions as I juggle my normal life activities along with the added responsibility of caring for my husband. My life resembled a carrousel at the county fair ---up and down, round and round. The real issue was I could not find the controls to turn it off. Sometimes, my sheer exhaustion and doubts kept me wondering if I would get through these adversities. The rigors of giving care were emotionally draining and frightening.

In the pages of this book I have inserted newsletters I wrote to our family and friends journaling the transplant procedure. Our story will give you a clear picture of what it was like being a caregiver through these experiences. You will see my struggles as I tried to make sense of what was happening. These adversities forced me to confront my inner state. I will share from my heart my doubts and fears when things were not going so well, and I will take you to the mountaintops of victories as God gave peace and hope found only in my personal relationship with Jesus Christ. He became the object of my faith during this journey as I learned to trust Him during the challenges and difficult times. At that depth of human hopelessness, I discovered the strength and sufficiency of God's Grace. Not until I discovered that the situation was more than I could handle and that my life as well as Bill's were out of my control did I discover that life is securely in God's control. I experienced some great lessons that can only be learned while living in a pit.

I want you to read this when you need encouragement to get through an adversity intact. Some of you will face cancer as a patient or a caregiver, and others will meet different challenges, struggles, and disappointments in life. Perhaps a stem cell transplant is an option that you may want to consider. Whatever you are going through God can use those circumstances to conform you to His image. Let Him take His sandpaper and make something worthwhile out of a difficult situation.

CHAPTER 1

God, You Got My Attention

I find the document tucked in a side pocket of my husband's briefcase as I sit alone in our two-room Houston apartment that December night of 2006. Less than a mile away, my husband sleeps in a hospital bed. As my eyes scan the bold print at the top of the legal-sized paper, I wonder why I have not seen this one before. It has been placed behind the others. I quickly scan the other sheets of paper, reliving that emotional experience when Bill signed those documents declaring his "last will and testament" and giving me the power and authority to handle any legal matters, including health care. But this one is different. It has the word *declaration* written at the top. As I read, my eyes fill with tears, making the words on the page waver. I close my eyes, willing myself to gain control. Bill has written a personal legacy statement to be read if he should die.

It reads: "Having enjoyed a wonderful, blessed life in this earthly body, I look longingly for a city not made with hands, eternal in the heavens, where my glorious Savior awaits my coming. Being born again as a child of nine, I repented of my sins and placed my faith in the Lord Jesus Christ. I acknowledge God's sovereign grace upon my life and publicly declared Christ as my Lord and Savior. Over the years, I have experienced unusual joys and sorrow but have been wonderfully sustained by the grace and mercy of a loving heavenly Father." Tears quickly run down my checks as I finish reading every sentence declaring his love for me, our children, and our grandchildren.

Wiping my tears with a dishcloth from the kitchen table, I sit motionless as I think about all we are about to face. Bill and I both know this stem-cell transplant will be risky, but this is our only option. My thoughts drifted back over the past years as a thousand unspoken questions paraded through my mind. I know in my heart we are doing the right thing, but still an element of uneasiness remains. The apprehensions about the outcome had continued to capture my mind, keeping me in an emotional upheaval. What the end results will be, I do not know, but I know I have a powerful God who can and has accomplished lofty things. The past years have proven that to be true.

1

Eight Years Earlier

In late November 1998, Bill noticed an unpretentious lump about the size of a small grape on the left side of his neck. He probably would not have given the lump much thought except his brother, Dave, had been diagnosed with non-Hodgkin lymphoma two years earlier. Bill felt the need to have the lump checked.

His doctor told him, "It looks like you have an infection. I'm going to put you on an antibiotic. This should take care of the swelling. Come back and see me in two weeks."

Feeling reassured by the doctor's diagnosis and by my husband's always-healthy state, I had no reason to think of missing my upcoming business trip to San Diego. Meanwhile my intuitive husband scheduled a biopsy in Nashville. Having been married for three decades plus, he knew I would have terminated my trip if I had known of the scheduled procedure. Bill later told me he just had a feeling that something was wrong, even though his doctor did not feel the biopsy necessary. Our youngest son accompanied his dad for the removal of the lump. Following the simple procedure, the surgeon entered the outpatient recovery room, and almost immediately Bill knew by the doctor's body language that the news would not be good.

The usually upbeat doctor had a shocked and somber look on his countenance as he shifted from side to side. Whatever report he had, he obviously didn't want to say it. Bill's suspicions were confirmed.

Dressed in his white physician's jacket with his hands clasped together, the apologetic doctor said, in his monotone voice, "Mr. Betts, I have some bad news for you. You have cancer. I'm so sorry. I had no idea the node would be cancerous, but it is."

A long pause followed, one appearing to last forever.

Finally, my optimistic husband said, "What do we do next?"

The doctor replied, "I'm going to send the biopsy to the pathologist so the lymph node can be studied under a microscope. I will give you a call when I have the final results."

The surgeon shook Bill's hand and left the room. The news had been delivered. Bill had the rest of the week to process the information before I returned from my trip. He decided not to tell me over the phone but to wait for my arrival.

Whenever Bill and I have been apart for awhile, our homecoming becomes a special celebration. Turning toward the last exit from the concourse, I saw Bill standing amid the crowd. There he stood, my tall, handsome husband. I picked up my pace as my feet moved swiftly toward him. I threw my arms around him, embracing him passionately. The scent of Calvin Klein's

Eternity cologne still lingered on his body as I squeezed tighter. Bill's strong arms surrounded me. My heart skipped a beat as he kissed me and I felt his smooth-shaven cheeks. I never like to be apart from my husband, especially this lengthy past week with so many miles between us. He held my hand gently as we moved in sync toward the luggage area.

Bill surprised me with a scrumptious dinner and time together at one of my favorite Italian restaurants. While eating several servings of salad, yummy bread sticks, and a plateful of pasta and chicken marsala, Bill and I talked about our week, especially how our children were doing. I had spent a couple of extra days with our oldest son who lived in California so I expounded on all of our sightseeing adventures. Bill and I stayed in our corner booth quietly sipping our coffee and talking together until the sun went down. Tears glistened briefly in the corner of my eyes as Bill held my hand and we exchanged our words of love for each other. Our time of sharing renewed our kindred unity of oneness.

Later that evening after I unpacked and deposited my dirty clothes in the downstairs hamper, Bill took my hand in his as we sit on the side of the bed.

"Barbara, I have something I need to tell you."

I thought, *We have been talking nonstop for the past two hours. What else could he possibly want to convey?* The previous smile on his face changed to a serious expression as he recounted the biopsy.

Suddenly, a word I must have heard a thousand times before rushed over me with tidal-wave force. Bill drew me close. I felt the warmth of his body as he cuddled me. My breath rushed out so rapidly, I felt as if my chest might collapse. I sucked great gulps of air, attempting to calm myself. But tears clouded my vision as I choked back a sob. My heart was catapulted into my throat as I tried to speak; but my tongue, taken captive by fear, submitted to silent paralysis. Hour-long minutes passed before I could think again, speak again. As I sat mute, my gaze pinned to Bill, he reached for my hand. The need to understand overwhelmed me.

"It's going to be all right, Barbara. It's OK," I heard from a distance, as he stroked me reassuringly, steadily drawing me back to the safety of our shore.

Bill lifted my hand to his lips as he prayed aloud. As I listen to my husband's calming, pastoral voice, I felt a gradual releasing of the apprehension that so quickly engulfed me only moments ago.

Bill prayed, "God, You are in control of our lives. This cancer is bigger than anything we have ever faced. Give us the grace and strength as we proceed down this unknown path that our eyes will remain focused on You." I took a calm breath as Bill continued to pray. "God, show Barbara Your love tonight as we rest in Your presence." Bill's prayer lasted only a short minute, for our emotions carried the rest of the conversation. No words can fully capture the moment. I'm so glad God knows our innermost thoughts and emotions even when we cannot speak them.

Bill, exhausted from the weight of a weeklong burden and the relief of finally sharing his load, fell into a deep sleep almost the second his well-creased cheek hit the pillow. He slept soundly. But for me the night lingered, a night of tossing and turning. Many thoughts rolled through my mind like tumbleweeds across the prairie without direction or control. I cannot make any sense of what I have heard. Bill has always been in good physical shape. He never even gets a cold or cough. The only time he was pale was when he had to change our children's diapers or clean up after one of their throw-ups. It never failed, as soon as Bill put on his freshly ironed Sunday shirt, with his sermon ready, diaper bag in tote, one of our babies would decided to spit up, and guess who would be holding this offspring? Their daddy! The smell turned his stomach sour potentially making him gag and becoming the next one to throw up.

Last year Bill and I rode our bikes in the Smoky Mountains of East Tennessee. I could hardly keep up with his pace and match his energy level. I became Wiley Coyote trailing behind my Road Runner husband. Halfway through our mountain trek, I needed a knee replacement and a pacemaker, as Bill, looking fresh as a babe just birthed from a mountain spring, simply smiled as he rehydrated with a bottle of water.

I remembered reading the statistic that one out of three people will eventually get cancer. But I never thought my vigorous husband would have this serious health problem. Cancer is always something other people have. This cannot be happening to us. Having served in several churches as pastor and wife, Bill and I have ministered to families who have been touched by cancer. We have listened to cancer patients' stories, their fears, and their hopes. We have prayed that God would heal them physically, emotionally, and spiritually. Together we have lovingly guided families that have been affected by cancer to God, the strong Rock during times of crisis.

Bill and I have visited and held the hands of loved ones and even been there when life ended prematurely because cancer took its toll on a young teenager. We have seen families suffer great adversity and brokenness. I remember a husband asking this question, "Why do good people suffer?" as he stood beside his dying wife and mother of three young children. I couldn't answer that question that day, and I still don't know the answer many years later. My human understanding struggles to make sense of why bad things happen in life, the ups and downs, the twists and turns, and those heartaches, pain, and disappointments. Now my family will be going down a path where I don't know what lies ahead. We will have to come to grips with this awful sickness that can slowly destroy the body and bring a plethora of emotions.

The diagnosis must be wrong. Maybe it is really not cancer. This must be a terrible mistake. Salty tears began rolling down my cheeks.

"God, make this nightmare go away," I silently cried.

As Bill continued to sleep, I continued to dream up nightmares. All kinds of images flooded my mind—nausea, vomiting, hair loss. Questions kept bouncing off the bedroom ceiling. How sick will Bill get? Will he be able to work? Will I be able to care for him? What if he dies? How would I ever live without my soul mate? God, do You really love me?

I allowed the tears to flow as I poured out my questions mingled with regrets and requests. I began to plead with God, desperately reasoning my case.

"Lord, You know I have tried to raise our children in Your ways, to be a faithful parent. I have made mistakes even in my marriage, but those are behind me now. Bill and I are looking forward to being an empty-nest couple, but now this cancer. Why now when life has been going so well? Have I done something wrong? I'll do whatever, just make this go away."

The hours passed. I cried out to God, and somehow a small candle of hope lit my heart. I felt a gradual calming peace come over me. I have always heard adversity will bring one back to dependence on God. God had gotten my attention. In the quietness of the night, I thought about the words Jesus said on many occasions, "Don't be afraid; trust Me." I remembered a verse from Psalms: "When I am afraid, I will trust in you" (Ps. 56:3).

I heard God speaking to me, not in an audible voice but in my mind. He comforted me with His peace by reminding me to take courage. "I've told you all this so that trusting me, you will be unshakable and assured, deeply at peace. In this sinful world you will continue to experience difficulties. But take heart! I've conquered the world" (John 16:33, *The Message*).

I felt stronger. The awareness of God's presence gave me strength and the knowledge that God has conquered the world, including cancer.

With a weak but renewed boldness, I said, "I will experience this difficulty with unshakable assurance because my trust is in Christ."

What a calming realization those words had on me. God replaced my uncertainties with His peace. God wanted me to trust Him with this cancer. I finally took a deep breath and relaxed. Closing my eyes and envisioning God's arms around me, I fell asleep at last.

CHAPTER 2

Watching and Waiting, the Hard Stuff

Daylight peaked through the window as I heard my husband move around the bedroom. Bill had been up before dawn in his study. Contrary to his early schedule, I'm not a morning person. I like to sleep in, especially this day since my tossing and turning lingered way into the night hours. I slowly opened my eyes, adjusting to the light. Bill came to the side of the bed. He knew it had been a rough night for me.

"Barbara, we're gonna get through this just fine," Bill said as he kissed my forehead. "How about a cup of coffee? I'll meet you downstairs." Bill's positive attitude has always helped me have a more optimistic view of difficult situations. Seated on the edge of the bed, I took a deep breath and leaned forward, moving into the start of a new day.

Every time the phone rang, I jumped, waiting for the official diagnosis from Bill's doctor. No one seemed in a hurry. But I went about my usual morning tasks, amazed I could still function. Waiting for the call made me edgy. I silently kept hoping just maybe this is all a mistake.

Several days passed before the surgeon delivered the final pathology report. I sat close as Bill held the receiver between us. "Bill you have non-Hodgkin lymphoma." The surgeon gave the name of an oncologist for Bill to contact. I leaned back on the couch speechless. How could two brothers come up with the same type of cancer? First Dave, now Bill!

I asked Bill, "Do you think this cancer connects back to something in your childhood or early environment?" Bill grew up in a suburb of St. Louis, Missouri, with his parents and four brothers in a small two-bedroom, one-bathroom house heated with coal. The boys took turns filling the furnace during those wintry snowy days. The family has always been close, but Dave and Bill are just three years apart and shared numerous sports and activities during their childhood days.

Bill said, "I doubt there is any connection, but you never know for sure."

It crossed my mind that perhaps those many wrestling matches, sharing the same bottle of Coke, or eating off the same plate contributed in some way as a connection. When one does not have all the answers, unrealistic assumptions enter your thinking. With all those many unanswered questions, I determined right then to learn all I could about this cancer and, if possible, make it go away. With my life on the brink of being turned upside down, I needed to do something. I wanted a fix for this intruder into our lives.

I have always been a fixer. It's my motherly nature. When one of our three children scraped a knee or had a booboo, mom always knew how to fix it. I would tell them, "This is not going to hurt," while I put ointment on the spot, carefully blowing air on the exact point of injury. "Let me kiss it, and I'll make it well," I would say, as if I had magic saliva or something to kiss and blow away the owie. Next came the Band-Aid and all was well. Mom, the caregiver, had fixed it.

This booboo called cancer was going to be much more difficult for this caregiver. I knew I couldn't fix it! Let me just go back to fixing little scrapes and cuts, back to where I had been before I heard the word cancer. I couldn't just kiss away this hurt. Feeling trapped by this new circumstance life had thrown our way, I wasn't sure even how to begin to fix the situation. How could I fix this when I could not even make sense of what was happening?

Why do oncologists think that if they can give you enough cancer pamphlets your questions will be answered? The medical pamphlets are filled with all those hundred-dollar words nonmedical people don't understand. "Just what is follicular B-cell lymphoma?" I ask Bill as we sorted through the medical terms. "And what about this Hodgkin and non-Hodgkin name? Sounds like a Mr. and Mrs. name instead of types of lymphoma." I read that about 12 percent of people with lymphoma have Hodgkin Lymphoma. The rest have non-Hodgkin lymphoma. Bill was in the majority group.

Information is a powerful ally when a loved one has cancer. I needed to learn all I could about this type of cancer plus all the possible treatment options available, including clinical trials. After researching what seemed like volumes of information, I developed this simple understanding about Bill's cancer. Remember, this is a laywoman's description on this subject not an experienced doctor's interpretation.

Lymphoma is cancer that begins in cells of the immune system. The word lymphoma is the name for a group of cancers that start in the lymphatic system. I recalled studying about the lymphatic system in my high school science class. It's part of the bigger immune system involving the lymph nodes. The immune system is critical for survival because we live in a world full of ugly, harmful germs that have the potential to become chronic diseases.

Without an immune system our bodies would be unable to fight off illness. The white blood cells are the body's foot soldiers sent throughout the body to destroy the enemy called infection. If the white cells change a certain way, they become abnormal and are then called lymphoma cells. Bill's white cells had become abnormal, which meant that his body's fighting warriors, his immune system, would be weakened and hindered in their ability to protect him from certain viruses and infections.

The cancerous cell is not content to be just one cell; it wants to multiply. And before long the cells pile up, and form cell masses. These masses gather in the lymph nodes, which would account for Bill's enlarged node. If a person has cancerous lymph nodes, his immune system is in jeopardy, making the body unable to resist infections, which could lead to earthly death. It sort of reminds me of the spiritual cancer cell called sin. A sin can multiply, and before long it piles up in our lives making our appearance ungodly. If sin is not atoned by the blood of Jesus Christ, eternal death will result.

Daily confession of sins is our ongoing treatment plan for those spiritual cancers that so easily enter our lives. "If we confess our sins, He is faithful and just to forgive us our sins and to cleanse us from all unrighteousness." John 1:9. Sin can drain our spiritual power; confession restores it. Just like spiritual cancer, physical cancer needs a treatment plan to remove it from the body. If not removed, it will infect and destroy the body. That was the scary part. I wanted to say to those cancerous cells: "Get out of my husband's body. You are not going to take up residence in it!" I found God's treatment plan for sin, and now I needed a treatment plan for this cancer.

Since these unwelcome intruders can pick and choose where they want to go, they had decided to show up in other parts of Bill's body, even putting their footprints in his bone marrow. Bill's follicular B-cell lymphoma was a slow-growing type, also called low grade or indolent. Some patients with fast-growing lymphomas can be cured, but with slow-growing lymphomas, treatment can keep the disease in check for many years, but even remissions last only a short time.

Bill's brother, Dave, had a fast-growing kind of lymphoma, so after surgery with treatments, his cancer went into remission. However, Bill's cancer was the slow-growing kind with no cure and considered advanced to stage IV, meaning the lymphoma was widespread in all parts of the body, including those traces in his bone marrow.

In the world of cancer, the stage of a cancer at diagnosis is important. In the past nearly all stage IV cancers were considered medically incurable. Because Bill's cancer was indolent, it grew slowly in the beginning. Due to Bill's age and because he had no other medical problems, his oncologist said,

"Bill, we are not going to start you on treatments at this time. Come back in three months for your checkup, and then I will see what we need to do."

What! I couldn't believe what I just heard! My husband had just been diagnosed with cancer, and his oncologist wanted to take a "wait and watch" approach. I wanted a treatment plan. This did not compute in my mind. I was born with an impatient temperament, and having to wait has never been easy for me. I'm always looking for the quick-fix solution that resolves all situations and removes all hurts. For example, I cannot wait the forty-five minutes for dinner to bake in the conventional oven, so I stick it in the microwave for five minutes.

My lack of patience goes back to my childhood days and has carried over into my adult life. It really manifested itself during the holiday seasons. I've never told my own children about this for fear they would do this as well, but here's my confession. I could not wait till Christmas morning to open my presents, so as an eight-year-old I quietly made my way to the living room where the presents were hidden. While my mom and dad were sleeping, I softly tiptoed to the closet with a flashlight, removed the tape, and carefully unwrapped my gifts, took a look, then rewrapped them. My mother never wrapped the presents tightly so she could not tell I had sneaked a peek! My vocabulary did not have the word *wait*, but over a lifetime I would learn some great lessons from the *wait* word. The Lord knew this was an area in which I needed help.

Numerous opportunities to test my patience came rather quickly as Bill and I traveled back and forth for those doctor's appointments, waiting in the examination room. No one seemed to be in a hurry. It didn't make sense to me. Bill had cancer, but nobody did anything. Everyone, including me, was watching for any changes in Bill's body that would indicate the need to start treatment. I could not see much change in outward appearances the first year, but inside Bill's body those dormant cancer cells were slowly beginning to awaken, increasing in size and becoming active. The initial period of wait and see was over. Bill's oncologist started the first series of treatments the second year.

Knowing I needed to be schooled in scores of lessons involving patience, God gave me many opportunities during the next seven years. Bill eventually received more than one hundred chemo treatments. There have been times those years of treatments seemed like an eternity. Some days I felt imprisoned by the grip this cancer had on us and the uncertainty of what the treatment outcomes would be. I desperately wanted it to be over, but this disease would not go away. As the disease progressed, the treatments became more frequent and powerful, leaving Bill with chronic fatigue. Our lives had definitely changed. Each chemo regimen would keep the cancer in check for three to six months. When the cancer flared up, treatments would start again; likewise my tutorial classes continued on to the next level of tolerance.

As I watched anxiously year after year, hoping for remission but only seeing a disease progress, I found it easy to question God's timing. However, I knew in my heart God's timing is always right. Timing and patience can be expressed as learning to accept difficult situations from God without giving Him a timeline to remove them. If my husband had been cured or put into remission during those early years, I would not have learned what I needed to learn. From that perspective it would have been tragic. I need not be so presumptuous as to criticize the providence of God when it appears to procrastinate. I'm still learning God's timing is always right and He always has much to teach me about His ways during those wait-and-watching periods.

God wanted to build character in my life, and He planned to use my husband's cancer for the purpose making of me more like Him. These trials including the watching and waiting were a part of the refining and shaping process that burns away impurities and prepares me to meet Christ and to be a reflection of His image. First Peter 1:6–7 (NLT) says, "So be truly glad. There is wonderful joy ahead, even though you have to endure many trials for a little while. These trials will show that your faith is genuine. It is being tested as fire tests and purifies gold—though your faith is more precious than mere gold. So when your faith remains strong through many trials, it will bring you much praise and glory and honor on the day when Jesus Christ is revealed to the whole world." As gold is heated, impurities float to the top and can be skimmed off. Likewise this cancer became the heat to be use by God to refine and strengthen my faith.

What the textbooks taught me about this cancer was mere medical science. But what God would teach me was more than watching a disease progress, for He would strengthen me spiritually, preparing me for not only what was to come in the years ahead but also what He intended to produce in my life. God knew all these experiences would help me to be more patience, and patience would create Godly traits. God would use these adversities to produce character, which is a life that is approved, tested, and qualified as genuine. Christian character is the evidence of God working within me to produce His likeness and image. Romans 5:2–4 says, "And we rejoice in the hope of the glory of God. Not only so, but we also rejoice in our sufferings, because we know that suffering produces perseverance; perseverance, character; and character, hope."

Yes, watching and waiting are hard stuff, but the rewards are most beneficial. The Lord is good to those who wait for Him.

CHAPTER 3

Life Is More Than "Happily Ever After"

The sights and sounds of the long narrow treatment room are recognizable to me as I accompany Bill for his many chemo treatments. Patients hooked up to IVs receiving their chemotherapy can sit in one of the ten brown recliners positioned around the room. The saline-solution bags are hanging on movable poles as the contents dribble through the tubing connected to the patients' veins. Today an ever-present sound, ka-lug, ka-lug, intersperses the silence, reminding me of the importance of the IV machines as they distribute the cancer-fighting drugs. Some of the machines begin to beep detecting air in the line, or the cycle is over. The monotonous pattern of the wall clock's ticking keeps patients aware of the time. The hands of the clock move, yet for some patients life appears to stop.

Two nurses work the treatment room attending to the patients needs and making sure IVs are flowing continuously like water through a straw. The large window across the front side of the room on the ninth floor suite of Baptist Hospital reveals Nashville's skyscrapers in the background. The sun shining through the windows gives off a glow of comfort as patients share their stories. I am amazed at how well some sick people can look and feel while going through such toxic treatments. Do not get me wrong, cancer is no picnic, and a few patients do look thin and ill while others look tired and afraid. In the midst of all their struggles, there is always a hope for a cure and a better day.

Bill has his favorite recliner next to the door. I sit next to him in an uncomfortable straight-back chair while Bill tries to relax in the cushioned lounger with a pillow and blanket to knock off the chill. Televisions are positioned on the wall, but we bring books from home. Bill reads only about four pages before he drifts in and out of sleep. I'm amused as I watch his eyes fighting to stay open only to succumb to what I know happens each time he gets chemo. I often think maybe the nurses add a little sleeping medicine to the chemo. Actually, the benedryl given to Bill to offset any side effects keeps him resting peacefully. As Bill sleeps and the hours pass, I close my book and allow my mind to race back to 1969, the year I met Bill.

Bill's reddish blond hair and charming smile matched the freshness of the colorful hints of gold appearing on the trees that sunny September afternoon. Meeting Bill and the months following would ultimately forever change my life's direction similar to the events that took place earlier that year when the first man set foot on the moon. *Apollo 11* Astronaut Neil A. Armstrong spoke those famous words, "That's one small step for a man, one giant leap for mankind." That single event brought the American people together in spite of the Vietnam War issues that continued to divide our nation. The moon landing showed our nation enormous challenges could be met and overcome.

Likewise, Bill would face gigantic challenges as he sought to win my heart, for I had a stubbornness that needed conquering. I'm glad Bill had a lot of patience and persistence as he pursued my affection. The significance of the first man on the moon would be nothing compared to the magnitude of what God would do as a result of Bill's coming into my life.

God would bring two people together, one from Missouri and the other from Texas. It would be one small step full of many challenges and one giant leap for a couple with a united purpose. As a teenager looking out my bedroom window viewing the sky with all its bright shining stars, I allowed my imagination and sweet dreams to carry me to the moon, dreaming of the future and the man I would one day meet and marry. The landing on the moon and the reality of a young girl's dream were about to happen.

Bill and I were both first-year students at Southwestern Baptist Theological Seminary in Fort Worth, Texas. I had just finished working in Lubbock, Texas, as an assistant Baptist student director at Texas Tech University, my first job after graduating from college. Now two years later, I had loaded my red Volkswagen Beetle with all my earthly possession to pursue a graduate degree in social work. I had a mission. My brother had joined the Peace Corps, and I would prepare to work in the field of Christian social services. I wanted to make a difference in this world.

It seems like only yesterday when I first saw Bill on that beautiful fall day. The sound of a car radio playing amid the laughter of voices got my attention as I turned toward the street in front of my dorm building. The guy driving the shiny, fire-engine red 1963 Pontiac convertible had just shoved his bangs away from his eyes. I remember the youthful smile on his face as the convertible turned the corner. The car was packed with students including two girls perched on the upper backseat.

I must admit my first impression of Bill had no resemblance of love at first sight. Bill reminded me of several freshman students I had previously worked with on the campus of Texas Tech. Their main focal point centered on having fun instead of scholarly pursuits. Bill appeared rather young and carefree as he proudly drove his convertible. I wondered about his motives for coming to this institution of higher learning, definitely not as focused as I would be on my studies. I had no time for what I witnessed as foolish horseplay, riding around campus trying to impress people with his convertible as if he were the grand marshal of Macy's Thanksgiving parade. My arrogant attitude would be one of the challenges Bill would confront.

I bumped into Bill the next day at the campus post office. He nodded and smiled. His smile intrigued me; however, I kept on moving in the direction of the door, giving him little recognition. I met Bill two days later at a campus cookout for new students. Throughout the evening students were encouraged to walk around the group and introduce ourselves to one another.

I had just taken a bite of my hotdog when someone came up from behind. I turned and there he stood, the convertible guy. "Hi, my name is Bill Betts. I'm from St. Louis, Missouri. Tell me, Barbara, where are you from." I thought, *I don't recall telling him my name.* I had not introduced myself, so how did he know my name? We had a short conversation, and I quickly moved toward the fire pit where other students stood. The flashback of the boy in the convertible with his entourage of girls still lingered.

By the end of the night, I had managed to avoid Bill, especially since my girlfriend had whispered in my ear she had heard Bill might have an interest in dating me. I did not want to give Bill any impression I shared his feelings, so you might say I absolutely gave him the cold shoulder. Besides I had met someone more interesting, not this guy from the "Show Me State."

In addition to being a full-time student, I had taken a job as director of women's work at an intercity mission located in the middle of a housing project where I also taught a morning preschool class three days a week. This became a perfect place for some of my clinic practices as well as working at a nearby facility for unwed mothers.

On Sundays I attended the mission church along with about seven other seminary students who volunteered their time. The first Sunday I looked across the pew, and there Bill sat. He nodded and smiled. *How did he know this is the church I would be attending?* I wondered, trying, instead of thinking about Bill, to concentrate on the service.

Two Sundays later, Bill joined the mission church and immediately started working with teenagers and families living in the nearby housing project. We were linked in ministries along with the other seminary students as we planned and implemented many outreach activities for the church. Now our paths would crisscross often, but I continued to keep my distance, making clear by my actions Bill would be just a friend, nothing more, especially since my close friend now had an interest in Bill. I gave Bill absolutely no reason to think his dating interest in me would be reciprocated. He later told me I had been rather snobbish, high and mighty. He finally showed less interest in asking me for a date. We just shared our common friendship.

Over the next six months God began to work on my pretentious attitude, and I began to see Bill in a different light. Bill and I never had classes together, but we saw each other frequently on campus. He always had his friendly smile behind those polite kind words as we passed each other. Often we would eat at the same table during mealtimes discussing profound theological thoughts. I witnessed Bill's deep convictions, values, and beliefs. My snobby and standoffish actions toward him begin to melt as I saw a multilayered person behind those big brown eyes and that suntanned convertible glow. I will forever remember two specific times God used to change my view of Bill.

The first time Bill preached at the mission, I heard a man full of godly wisdom. He proclaimed the Word of God with boldness and clarity. No doubt God had called Bill to the preaching ministry. He shared the Word with a deep personal confliction. My heart felted the touch of God's Spirit as I listened. To hear Bill pray seemed like being in the presence of God. He appeared to live in uninterrupted communion with God. Bill became a great inspiration to me. His ideals were terrific, and he lived up to them. I saw in him someone who always carried with him, and therefore gave to others, a sense of the authority of God. His life was truly Spirit filled, and his one burning passion was devotion to his Savior.

Hearing Bill preach blessed me, but even more would be seeing how he daily lived out what he preached. Working side-by-side at the mission gave me many opportunities to see him in action. We made visits with families in the housing project. Bill's kindness and down-to-earth talk always demonstrated respect for these families who faced various difficult situations. He saw them as real people, not just someone to help. He cared for them and took the time just to be with them.

Whether he was playing football with a teenager or helping a grandfather with his truck engine, he always made people feel at ease. He did not mind if his hands got greasy and dirty. If he had a job to do, he would finish it. He played with the children and was never happier than when crawling around on the floor playing at being a tiger or a lion, led triumphantly by a small boy or girl whom he allowed to tease him.

The second incident that gave me a new perspective of Bill occurred when several seminary students were delivering food baskets to families. We were invited to stay awhile at one of the homes. Soon after we settled on a small worn couch, the young mother held out her newborn baby for Bill to hold.

Bill did not hesitate; he stood to receive the infant from the mother. He held the child in his arms like a guy would hold a football, with such confidence and ease. His comfort level and gentleness amazed me as he cooed and quieted the crying baby. I knew immediately, this man would make a great father. I later learned he had ample experience with small children coming from a sizable family with an abundance of nieces and nephews.

I don't know the exact date or time my attraction for Bill began to blossom, but it happened. I had many opportunities to spend time with him in group settings, but now I wanted to date Bill. When I looked at Bill with those big, brown eyes, something inside of me melted. I found him charming and irresistible. Just seeing Bill excited my heart and awakened new emotions of desire unlike anything I had ever felt. The pounding of my heart was an indication of excited delight every time my eyes would meet his. I wanted our friendship to be more. I had fallen in love with Bill.

Those months of friendship had given me time to know Bill, and now I wanted more than anything else to be with this mature man God had brought into my life. He had all the qualities I had dreamed about. But how could I let Bill know my desire to date him especially since I had strongly conveyed I wanted just a friendship, putting a stop to all his earlier advances? A mutual friend helped solve my dilemma by letting Bill know that if he asked me for a date, I would gladly accept.

I not only accepted that first Saturday night date but also Bill's proposal of marriage seven days later. You might say we had a short courtship; however, I had no doubt when Bill took my hand and said, "I want to spend the rest of my life with you. I love you." To which I reply, "I love you. I guess that means we need to get married if you want to be with me for life."

Years later Bill's account of the story was somewhat different. He says I was the one who proposed marriage. Regardless of whose side you believe, the one thing I'm sure about is when Bill kissed me that unforgettable night I knew my heart was his forever. Our friendship had turned to love. That friendship was the key in providing a sound base for a marriage relationship.

Four months later Bill and I were married in the chapel of my home church. Our wedding day was one of the happiest of my life. I walked down the church aisle knowing that I was walking into my future. One which beckoned to the longing of my heart, yet included many unknowns. I remember that day, as if it were yesterday. I was seeing the hope and the excitement I had always dreamed this day would hold. Bill and I pledged our love and commitment to each other before God, our friends and family.

As a young bride I thought my life was perfect. God had given me the most wonderful man for a husband. I felt so loved by Bill. We moved into the seminary deluxe housing for married students. It was an ideal, serene environment away from any troubles and woes of life. I felt protected. No hurt would come to me. Life was good. The dream I had dreamed about as a young girl had come true. All of my plans had worked out perfectly. In other words, I was going to live happily ever after.

Those newlywed years reminded me of the church camp where I asked Jesus Christ to come into my heart at the age of nine. The peaceful isolated site, miles away from the world, was a picture-perfect environment. The kumbaya campfires among the beautiful, undisturbed tall trees and breathtaking mountain peaks reflected a tranquil setting portraying my early concept of the Christian life. I knew I would forever be sheltered from adversity and harm. I thought God would make everything nice and pleasant. I would have no major problems because I was immune from the ills and troubles of this world.

I would soon learn differently. Life is full of bumps, potholes, and even washed-out bridges. God didn't promise that once I accepted Jesus as Lord and Savior and found the perfect soul mate, I'd be protected from harm, pain, and stress. Life is filled not only with that which is good and painless, but life can have troubles and heartaches. Tears and sorrow come to us all. They are part of living. Living is not in an isolated, safe-haven mountain environment. God never said the road of life would always be smooth and easy.

Having now been married over thirty-eight years, I know life may not always be what I would have wanted. Things happened in my life I never thought I would have to experience, but I have. I didn't like them and never imagined those things could occur in my life. I have learned from the Scriptures that Jesus experienced many sufferings while on this earth, and I will also not get out of this world without experiencing afflictions. Life is hard, and I may not always live on top of the mountains, but I have learned over these years that happiness and growth occur while you're climbing the mountain.

Those painful life trials may at times appear to be unfair, but no matter what the future days hold, I'm placing my belief in God. He not only controls each event of my life, but He is faithful in His love and will sustain me through everything—the good times as well as the tough times. Jesus Christ can ease the heartaches.

Somewhere between fond memories of my courtship and the beeping of the IV machine, I draw my thoughts back to the present. Today this treatment room is a part of my life. God has not promised to exempt me from hardship and affliction, and He never said I would live in a perpetual rose garden free of black spots and mold. Cancer is one of those ugly flowers. It is not something I wanted for my husband, but it is what we've got. I would not have chosen cancer for my husband, but God had other plans. The bag of chemo has slowly emptied its content. Another treatment is finished.

My husband's eyes open after a restful sleep. The peace on his face still lingers, and I reach for his hand. My convertible guy's optimistic outlook has always been the stalwart that has carried us through our years of marriage. Bill's strong faith has been a constant all his life, and he never seems to be discouraged, even through all of the chemotherapy. I whisper in his ear, "Thank you for being my husband. I love you my convertible guy."

CHAPTER 4

Every Day Has Its Good and Bad

The familiar eight by ten-feet examination room is cold this wintery December morning of 2003. I inch closer to Bill and wait for the doctor to enter. Bill makes me feel protected, as I rest my face against his shoulder. I study the blood report he holds in his hand. We both are silent as we stare at the paper. Bill's blood counts have dropped. I know what this means. The blood report will not be a Monopoly "get out of jail free" card. Instead, my husband will be captive to another round of chemo treatments even though it has only been three months since finishing the last treatment series. Days like this, the cold chill goes deeper than the goose bumps on my arms. Discouragement comes over me. I do not want Bill to see my disappointment, but I know he feels disheartened as well. I tell God, "I will trust you with this cancer problem." But at this moment those feelings of melancholy and doubt are besieging my heart, and I swallow back the tears.

The doctor enters the room confirming what I already suspect, bad news. "Bill, we need to start you on another round of treatments," the oncologist says. My eyes begin to sting. *Remain calm and stay strong*, I tell myself. The doctor goes on to say: "There is a new drug. We haven't tried this one. I believe it will help." He says it with such confidence. Where is my confidence? I can't pretend any longer. The magnitude of seeing my husband battle this ongoing fight with a cancer so stubborn it refuses to submit to any cancer-fighting drugs leaves me helpless.

Dealing with cancer treatments, the day-to-day occurrences of my life, and the fear of the unknown are keeping me in a cyclone of turmoil. My stress levels are peaking as I try to meet family needs, continue a full-time job, care for elderly parents who lived in other states, help with children and grandchildren, and now having my loved one battling another setback with cancer.

I feel like I'm a dog-paddling on the sea of life. I have been thrown into a body of water so deep I cannot keep my head above the water. Fighting to stay afloat but sinking fast, I'm exhausted. I pray: "Lord, how do I deal with all these happenings. How do I deal with another bad blood report?" This dark funnel cloud called cancer keeps engulfing my days, compounding an already full schedule, and emotionally draining me. I'm having some bad days.

Have you ever had a day that looks like this?

I awake realizing the alarm did not go off. I need to be at work in thirty minutes; however, I have a forty-five minute drive to the office. I quickly dress, forget the hair wash! It will just have to be a bad-hair day. I get in the car, putting on my makeup as I drive, hoping my lipstick is within my lip line. After sitting in traffic for twenty minutes, I finally arrive at work, late. At this point I realize I'm wearing my navy blue top with my black pants. I'm functioning with one contact lens because I haven't had time to replace the one I lost. This is the day I'm to facilitate a training session with fifty eyes on me. Maybe they won't notice my lack of professional attire for the day! This is turning out to be more than a bad hair day. It has the potential to be a very bad day.

The day certainly did not start out well, but maybe there is hope. As I close the door to my office, I take a deep breath inhaling the fresh air from the one open window near my desk. I clear my mind of all the many family concerns, and I began sorting through the stack of papers. I glance at my to-do list made the night before, proudly checking off each accomplishment as the morning passes. Unexpected situations always pop up that demand my attention, which necessitates flexibility. But today those work projects appear so overpowering that my brain calls out, "Can't multitask anything else, I'm in overload!" My supervisor needs this report completed. I've got this to do and this to finish. I wonder how I will ever get it all done.

With the help of three cups of coffee, I somehow managed to complete a few assignments in addition to leading the training workshop. In spite of the glaring looks regarding my unprofessional attire for the day, the workday finally comes to an end. I lock my office door, thankful that I made it through another workday. The drive home gives me an opportunity to ponder the day's events and realign my negative thoughts with God's positive Word. I love Romans 8:28, "And we know that God causes all things to work together for good to those who love God, to those who are called according to His purpose." I would certainly need that verse in light of what would happen next.

As I journey home, my cell phone rings. It's my daughter, Regina, on the other end. "Hey mom, can you pick up the kids? I've had an emergency, and I'm going to be running late," She asked rather quickly.

"Oh, sure honey, no problem." I reply. Oh, did I mention our daughter, her husband, Charles, and our two adorable grandchildren, Will, age three, and Kayelynn, age two, are living with us while their home is being built. Haley, the dog, came along as well. My husband and I have never had an animal to live inside our house. Nevertheless, concessions are made when we have the opportunity for grandchildren to live with us.

I pick up the children, rush home, let the dog out, and check the house like a poop detective to see if this cute little dog has done her thing on my floors. I'm relieved to see she has been a good little doggie. Surveying the piles of clothes on the floor, I quickly put in a load of clothes to wash. Our washing machine works overtime with the additional family members' dirty laundry to clean, plus a few extra items. Those weird noises are more frequent now since the stuffed teddy bear went through the cycle. I pat the top of the machine reassuring it this wash cycle contains only human clothes.

I turn toward the kitchen, opening the refrigerator door to get supper started. It's my turn to cook. I look through the shelves not finding the meat. I then realize I have forgotten to take the meat out of the freezer. At this point I'm not sure what we will eat, as I contemplate the option that my next house will have no kitchen, just vending machines and a large bulletin board with all the take-out restaurant numbers!

In the next thirty minutes I'm completely convinced this is not one of my better days. Haley, the dog, throws up on the living room floor. Kayelynn had given the dog some green play dough mixed with her cookie! As I'm on my knees gagging from the smell of the awful green substance the precious little dog has left on my carpet, Will, said, "Grandma, why is the floor wet?" He is pointing in the direction of the laundry room."

Rounding the corner I see to my horrid discovery, the washing machine water backing up into the downstairs toilet, overflowing. I quickly stop the washing machine and throw down every dry towel I can find while my grandchildren splash their feet in the soapy water. Proverbs 15:13 (NASB) says, "A joyful heart makes a cheerful face." My face did not look cheerful. How can I laugh at this day! And in the midst of all this I have a husband with cancer. Along with having a bad day, my heart ached.

After I finish drying the floor, Bill arrives home. He puts his arm around me and says. "Hope you had a good day today." A good day! I thought, *What does a good day look like? Lord, how can this be a good day with all of these happenings?* Caring for my husband, going back and forth to the hospital for treatments, and dealing with all of these unexpected events causes me to cry out. I don't like the way cancer has altered my life. As I am trying to juggle all of the normal life activities along with this added responsibility of caring for my loved one, I feel more like a sandwich than a human. I've become the slice of bologna sandwiched between all of these life situations.

As a young child, I would take my bologna sandwich and press it between my hands patting it down to a flat sandwich. Sometimes the mayonnaise would run out the sides of the bread, and I would lick it up like an ice cream cone. My mother would say that's not a ladylike way to eat a sandwich. Similarly, this crisis called cancer is pressing me flat, squeezing me, and I don't like it. It certainly has no sweet taste like ice cream or even the creamy mayonnaise; it has an unsavory taste.

I do not like the taste and the direction my life seems to be headed. These fast-track whirlwind demands and hectic days are pulling me in so many directions I feel my life reeling out of control. I am not sure how to keep the affairs of my entire family balanced. So I try to plan my day. Today is going to be a good one, but when things don't go the way I plan, like the bad blood report or the overflowing toilet, I get uptight. My plans aren't working out, so I even think I might not plan my days and just go with the flow! Actually, even if I plan out a day by saying, "I will have no plans," that would be a plan!

There are days I can identify with David in the Old Testament when he asked his soul, "Why are you cast down, O my soul? And why are you disquieted within me?" (Ps. 42:5, NKJV). David did a lot of talking to himself during some of his bad days. Likewise during my hectic days, I did some talking to God. I even have my own little pity parties where I learn a lot about Barbara. Some things I do not like about myself, especially the times when I accuse God of neglecting His care for me. I remember thinking these thoughts: *If God really loves me, He wouldn't allow all of this to happen to me. Why are my plans working out this way? Why am I having this bad day?*

What I learn through all of this is that I do not need to waste my time pitying myself or getting upset when plans do not work out the way I think they should. Neither do I need to blame God, pointing my bony finger at Him. Those thoughts will get me nowhere and only result in additional discouragement and gloom. Every day has its good and its bad. God is in the good days as well as the bad days, and He can use reversals to move me forward. God alone can determine what is truly good and what is truly bad. From God's perspective the bad days are really good days. He alone can use the bad to strengthen me, and that is good. Paul wrote in 2 Corinthians 4:16–18 (NKJV): "Even though our outward man is perishing, yet the inward man is being renewed day by day. For our light affliction, which is but for a moment, is working for us a far more exceeding and eternal weight of glory, while we do not look at the things which are seen, but at the things which are not seen. For the things which are seen are temporary, but the things which are not seen are eternal."

21

No matter how crazy my days become or how I feel about my situations, I make choices each day. I can choose how I will respond to whatever the day brings both the good and bad. My life will always include things that I have no control over. Some of those things will appear to be bad, but when I respond the way God intends for me to, I might just reap some blessings. I need to keep on keeping on and stay the course knowing God's hand is on my life.

As I care for my loved one, I will continue to experience firsthand the good and the bad, the joyous times, and even the painful disappointments, like bad blood reports. I may not like those uncontrollable day-to-day occurrences, but God is showing me that those situations I assess as bad days or events may ultimately be good. I do not need to prejudge the significance of good and bad any more than someone would prematurely judge the outcome of the sculptor whose art is unfinished. For what I believe is bad may turn out to be just what I need.

My Father will always do right so I can sing in the midst of both good and bad days. I can rejoice, for life's trials and afflictions might just be the best things that can happen to me!

CHAPTER 5

Living in My Circumstances

From the time Bill's treatments starting in the year 2000, he was able to tolerate the chemotherapy for next five years without too much difficulty. We lived a somewhat normal life in spite of our daily schedule changes. I am not sure I can describe a typical day, for my life resembled a carrousel at the county fair—up and down, round and round. The real issue was that I could not find the controls to turn it off.

I have always had a strong, self-sufficient spirit that insists on being in control. I like calling the shots and having the control panel at my side. I'm a great planner and can carry out most plans. I take pride when things go well but get frustrated when they don't. I would much rather tell God what I need than to have Him tell me what I need, especially when my life gets in those panic, frenzy stages of a runaway train. Despite my need for control, God had other plans. He wanted me to relinquish my control and let Him be the Engineer, the Mastermind at controlling the events in my life. He is certainly more intelligent, vigilant, and powerful than I could ever hope to be.

The Bible says that God has our times in His hand (see Ps. 31:15). During those days of living with cancer, God showed me that He, not Barbara, is in control—not the relentless cancer cells, not the toxic chemo, not the white-coated doctors, or the disarray of uncontrollable circumstances. As I surrendered control into the hands of a Sovereign God, living with cancer became easier.

The Betts household had numerous interruptions requiring many adjustments, for we definitely were in the cancer routine. The major changes to our routine came during the chemo cycles, as the chemo would flow endlessly through Bill's veins, week after week for months at a time. Life became demanding and tough. During those times I remembered what someone once told me, "When things get rough in life, it's the rubbing that brings out the shine." Sometimes I saw only a small glow shining through; however, in the midst of my darkness I learned lessons I might never have learned in the daylight.

The drug combinations became more toxic as the years passed. It was like putting poison in Bill's veins. I prayed, "Lord, let the chemo destroy the cancer cells but protect his good ones." Bill's treatments could last as long as eight hours or as short as one hour. On the longer days I would get our lunch at one of the local sandwich shops. Trying not to let our eating bother the other patients, we would move to a corner recliner, especially when some patients were experiencing nausea.

There were days Bill and I would take off from work, but for most of the treatment series we were able to go back to work after the treatments ended. Even if Bill felt awful, he tried to work some. He only missed days when he got so sick he could not function. My husband has a strong work ethic with a determined fortitude, and he had decided early in this cancer journey he would not let it interfere with his life.

I am thankful Bill never experienced many major discomforts. The antinausea medicines worked great. One drug actually turned his face beet red, starting with his ears and quickly moving across his cheeks. But for the most part he had few side effects he could not tolerate. An obvious change occurred as Bill's thick hair got thinner, but at this juncture in the journey, he had not completely lost it all, which helped his self-imagine. The real noticeable changes had to do with his level of energy. The chemo was sapping it.

Looking at Bill, you would not think he has a medically incurable cancer, but he does. When the lymph nodes enlarged, I knew Bill's cancer had flared up once again. The CT scans would confirm the tumors were growing, which meant another round of treatments. The lymph nodes were especially conspicuous in the neck area. Bill said, "My neck looks like a deer in rut." On that occasion Bill actually had no defined neck. The nodes had enlarged so much Bill looked like an NFL football player with a size twenty neck. Bill had to buy new shirts in larger neck sizes.

Occasionally, I noticed Bill struggling to concentrate. He told me that he had to read something several times in order to comprehend it. He had trouble remembering things, especially details from the past. He would forget the names of people he knew. When he struggled to recall things, he said, "I'm having my chemo moment."

When I forget something, I can only blame it on a senior moment. Since I have never experienced chemotherapy, I cannot use that excuse. Lately I have had memory loss regarding things from the past. For example, several years ago I had my fortieth high school reunion. The high school reunion committee sent a questionnaire for me to complete. They wanted information to use in a memory book, such as, "Tell your most memorable extracurricular activity in high school." It could be something I remembered about a day, a dance, a game, a place, a love, or a laugh. My recall functions are not what they use to be. My memorable high-school activities have long gone from my brain due to a malady called aging.

Maybe I am not as absentminded as the story of two elderly ladies who had been friends for many decades. Over the years they had shared all kinds of activities and adventures. Lately their activities had been limited to meeting a few times a week to play cards. One day as they were playing cards, the one looked at the other and said, "Now don't get mad at me. I know we've been friends for a long time, but I just can't think of your name! I've thought and thought, but I can't remember it. Please tell me your name." Her friend glared at her. For at least three minutes she just stared and glazed at her. Finally she replied, "How soon do you need to know?"

I am not quite at that stage. I still know my husband's name, and he knows mine. We do have handy name tags in the desk drawer for the future. Bill and I complement each other. What Bill forgets, I sometimes remember; and what I forget, Bill remembers. Is that not what married couples are supposed to do?

Besides the physical and mental challenges of living with cancer, families who are diagnosed with a life-threatening illness are confronted with emotional issues such as fear, depression, loneliness, anxiety, and even despair. Now I see those emotions close up and personal. I tried to play the bargaining game, which I think most caregivers do at some point in their journey.

Lord, if you will just heal Bill, I will . . . I've even thought, *If I could just do something special to earn or deserve healing from God* or, *If I could just be an especially good person, then God would reach down and heal my husband's cancer.* I realized cancer is not a punishment for bad behavior, nor is healing a reward for good conduct, and God's love for me has no strings attached. His love and presence in my life are not based on whether I am good enough because they are unconditional gifts.

Sometimes I wanted to run as far away as I could from the treatments Bill faced. Just as the psalmist said in Psalm 55:6–8 (NLT), "Oh, that I had wings like a dove! I would fly away and be at rest. Indeed, I would wander far off, and remain in the wilderness. I would hasten my escape from the windy storm and tempest."

Since I do not have wings, just give me a jet airplane, and I will go as far and as fast as I can from these circumstances called cancer. Just take me away from it all. Give me a box of facial tissues for my tears, and I will have my own pity party on my own little island. But, contrary to what I wanted, God chose not to take me out of my life's reality. His plan was for me to live in these circumstances. I will not be protected from the ravages of cancer, but God will protect me.

Many times I cried, and my emotional state became shaky as I attempted to process all that was happening. I did not always understand the circumstances, and I did not always see how any good could come out of these situations. When I found myself in those times of trial, that's when living got the hardest. I could not see clearly, much less understand. During those tough moments God said, "Trust Me." In my heart I knew God would see me through this even though from my view I could not make any sense of what was happening.

I must confess I struggled the most during this period of our life. I felted trapped in our impossible predicaments. My previous positive outlook and vision became blurry because I focused only on my emotions that kept me in fear of my circumstances. When my emotions controlled me, God would have to open my eyes so I could see my circumstances from God's perspective. Many time I needed a clear vision of the promise found in Romans 8:28 that God makes everything, even calamities, work for our good. Sometimes it's awfully hard to wait for the good to work. That is when God gently puts those drops of spiritual Murine in my eyes until my focus returns. I am reminded of Psalm 145:14 (TLB), "The Lord lifts the fallen and those bent beneath their loads."

God would give me a glimpse of His vision, allowing me to see these circumstances once again are ordained for His purposes. I may not fully see everything the way God can, but I have accepted the reality that these unchangeable circumstances are a part of God's design. I need to count my blessings instead of my calamities.

Here is a wonderful illustration on how God works. Someone sent me an e-mail called "When Your Hut's on Fire." The story talks about the only survivor of a shipwreck. He was washed up on a small, uninhabited island and continued to pray feverishly for God to rescue him. Every day he scanned the horizon for help, but none seemed forthcoming. Exhausted, he eventually managed to build a little hut out of driftwood to protect him from the elements and to store his few possessions.

One day after scavenging for food, he arrived home to find his little hut in flames, with smoke rolling up to the sky. He felt the worst had happened, and everything was lost. He was stunned with disbelief, grief, and anger, and He cried out, "God! How could you do this to me?" Early the next day he was awakened by the sound of a ship approaching the island. It had come to rescue him. "How did you know I was here?" asked the weary man to his rescuers. "We saw your smoke signal," they replied.

The moral of this story is that it is easy to get discouraged when things are going bad, but we should not lose heart because God is at work in our lives, even in the midst of our pain and suffering. I need to remember that story the next time my little hut seems to be burning to the ground. It just may be a smoke signal that summons the grace of God. Fear may keep me limping in the dark, but grace keeps me walking in the light. God has not promised He will always give me the answers and keep my hut from burning, but He has promised to give me His grace.

Like the survivor of the shipwreck. I have felt my hut on fire. I have prayed for God to rescue me. I have asked similar questions. Can anything good come out of this cancer? Why is this happening?

In pondering these questions, I thought about the process of baking a cake. I have baked numerous cakes in my lifetime. The finished product is always delicious, and everyone is eager to eat the cake. However, if I were to offer you some of the ingredients by themselves—"Have some cooking oil. Try this baking soda. How about a couple of raw eggs?"—you would say, "That is yucky!" Yes, you are right. All those things seem bad by themselves. But when they are put together in the right way, they make a wonderfully tasty cake!

God works in similar ways even though we may have difficulty seeing His ultimate plan and purposes while in the midst of a burning hut or a cake in progress. Many times I have wondered why He would let me go through such difficult times, but God knew what He was doing. The furnace of afflictions is for my protection and God's purposes. In those fiery flames of difficulties, I cried out to God, and He showed me His grace will always be sufficient.

While in college, I heard a preacher say that God has never promised the highway of life will always be smooth and easy. My life was experiencing many inevitable challenges as we progressed through the early years of living with cancer. Not only did I see how this disease was changing Bill's body, but other things were affecting me such as my outlook on life and my attitude about cancer. I saw that these circumstances were not meant to be lived in defeat, but I was to live them in victory.

Through these years with cancer, Bill and I have known many benefits and blessings. I do not need an airline ticket after all. If I fly away from these circumstances, I might just miss out on some of God's intended blessings and purposes.

CHAPTER 6

We're Not in This Journey Alone

In the spring of 2004, Bill's oncologist gave us the news, "Bill, your body is not responding to this last chemo regiment, and your blood counts are dropping. I think you may have developed myelodysplastic syndrome." He went on to say he would be making a referral to the Hematology Clinic at Vanderbilt Medical Center. If Bill had this syndrome, he could possibly be a candidate for a bone-marrow/stem-cell transplant. That was the first time Bill and I became aware of the possibility of a stem-cell transplant.

After the initial examination, the hematologist explained to us that myelodysplastic syndrome is a disorder of the bone marrow often associated with low blood cell counts requiring the need for transfusions. Bill had already had several blood transfusions this year. With this syndrome the bone marrow is not functioning normally and begins to produce immature blood cells. This disorder usually is found most often in adults over the age of fifty who have been exposed to excessive radiation. Bill had not had radiation; however, he had had large amounts of chemotherapy. Some toxic chemicals can also make a patient high risk for myelodysplasia, which is often called a pre-leukemia syndrome because patients with this have a significant increase in developing leukemia.

"Bill, I need you to have another bone-marrow biopsy so I can take a closer review of your bone marrow to be absolutely sure the information I have from your oncologist is correct and also to confirm the myelodysplastic." My husband's first reaction is "no way!" Just last week he had this test done, and he did not want to repeat this painful procedure. The uncomfortable images of the first procedure still lingered vividly in his mind. The oncologist drilling into his lower back, pushing down through the bone, literally positioning himself on top of Bill with full force extracting fluid from the bone marrow were just a few of the unpleasant scenes imbedded in his memory. The first experience left such an impression that even though he had had three other bone-marrow biopsies that were somewhat more tolerable since the first, the unpleasant memory definitely was hard to remove.

Bill's resistance and his determination were coming across loud and clear. "Is this really necessary?" he questioned the doctor. Dreading the test with a passion, the only way Bill would commit to another biopsy would be if the doctor completely knocked him out. My husband usually is a very cooperate patient, but when this test comes around, he is the biggest coward. He wanted no pain. So when the doctor agreed to give Bill some twilight injection allowing him to feel nothing, Bill finally but reluctantly agreed to the biopsy.

This is Bill's description of the above incident. He wrote in an e-mail.

This bone marrow biopsy has to be comparable to childbirth as far as the pain! I'm beginning to feel more like a laboratory rat than a patient. Reluctantly, I agreed that I would do the biopsy, but just before leaving the doctor's office, I gave twelve (count them, twelve!) vials of blood. Actually, I know how the cow feels when the farmer says she gave two gallons of milk. The cow didn't give the milk; the farmer took the milk! The doctor called later that evening to tell me my white count had increased to 1.9. I thank our Father that at least it was going the right way. Up! Obviously, the doctor was still very worried, so tomorrow I'll have the bone marrow biopsy.

The result of the bone marrow biopsy indicated Bill did not have myelodysplasis even though his white counts and other blood elements were continuing to be extremely low. The hematologist reminded Bill, "You need to be careful not to be around anyone who might be sick because you don't have much protection from infections." The words of caution have become familiar to us especially when Bill's white counts dropped. In spite of the low counts, Bill and I were encouraged by the bone marrow biopsy's results. Bill did not need the transplant.

Looking back on that experience, I see how we were protected in the circumstance. God needed us to wait for He was not ready for us to walk down the road of a stem-cell transplant even though this could have been the standard treatment strategy for Bill's disorder. God would have other paths for us to travel down in the next two years. He knew we needed to get some matters in order, and I also needed to learn some important lessons about trusting. God's timing is always right. The stem cell transplant would come later.

God was showing me that while He had not specifically answered my prayer regarding Bill's total healing, other prayers were indeed being answered. God promises to hear prayers, and He certainly responds faithfully to those prayer requests as His divine intervention becomes evident when God's people pray. I saw evidence of answered prayers when Bill's blood counts went from dangerously low to much improved counts, sometimes almost immediately. What seemed in the moment as hopelessness, God used to show His Divine involvement.

Bill wrote to our prayer partners regarding the results of the bone biopsy.

> I do believe in the power of prayer, so I asked my Bible study class and many others to pray for me that my white blood count would go up. I'm not always sure what the Lord has in mind for me relative to all this cancer stuff. Maybe I'll die with it, maybe I'll live with it. All I know for certain is that He who breathed life into me one day is the only One who can withdraw it from me. I'm comfortable with that and have been learning much in the meantime. I returned to the medical center where they drew more blood (only eight vials this time) and "enjoyed" another stimulating biopsy followed by a brief meeting with my hematologist. He basically said he would call me with the result of my bone marrow biopsy as soon as it came back. Finally last Wednesday evening he called to tell me the results verify that I do not have myelodysplasis at this time, but one puzzling report came back. My white count was normal. He had no explanation, admitted he did not know why this happened, but would continue to monitor my blood tests over the next several months. Now isn't that just like our Father to do exceedingly abundantly, above all that we ask or think.
>
> I returned to my oncologist last Friday for an examination, and as routine as clockwork they took blood. I'm happy to praise the Lord and report to you that my white count is still normal! My oncologist said he cannot account for my white blood cells being normal. He was sure I needed a bone-marrow or a stem-cell transplant and that's why he sent me to the hematologist. But what really had him puzzled is, you guessed it, there is no explanation as to why my white count is normal.
>
> I guess I'm just an enigma to my doctors at this time. I have tried to tell them about all the folks praying for me, but since you can't get that in a test tube, it's considered non verifiable. I rather enjoy being God's enigma. Well, so much for encapsulating my pilgrimage over the past several weeks. Please do continue to pray for me as they consider what treatment procedure to put me on

sometime within the next couple of weeks. My gratitude and love to all of your faithfulness in interceding on my behalf. May God return to you fourfold the blessing you have been to me.

Bill wrote this e-mail of praise and thanksgiving.

We are encouraged as we walk yet further down a road that is dimly lighted. Our trust and faith are anchored in a Rock, and the psalmist said it well, "You are my hiding place; You preserve me from trouble; You surround me with songs (shouts) of deliverance. I will instruct you and teach you in the way which you should go; I will counsel you with My eye upon you" (Ps. 32:7–8 NASB). With the Father's eye upon me, how can I not be filled with songs/shouts of praise and thanksgiving? He still has much to "instruct and teach" me in this way, but He assures me of His counsel. As more information comes I will keep you informed so you can pray as specifically and as effectually as possible. We send our love and thanks to each of you.

Bill's cancer is not curable, by the doctor's assessment, but that does not stop us from praying for total healing. I believe in the divine touch, and if God somehow wants Bill healed, He can do that. I'm learning to give Bill's cancer prognosis to the Lord, giving the Master of the universe permission to have His way in Bill's life. I have seen the power of prayer as many faithful prayer warriors lift Bill's daily needs to the throne of God. How wonderful to see time after time God's grace given as He answers those request. Bill's e-mails give testimony of God's divine interventions. Here's one from August 2003:

After learning four weeks earlier that my white blood count was down to .8 (needs to be between 5 and 7) I asked the Bible study class and numerous friends to pray for me. Today the blood report came back that my white count is now at 4.3! God did exceeding and abundantly above all I could have asked or thought. Psalm 57:2 says, "I will cry out to God Most High, To God who accomplishes all things for me."

Even the doctors were puzzled at how Bill's white cell counts would rise after being so low one week and then greatly improved the next. Bill wrote in an e-mail, June, 2004:

My doctor just called a few moments ago to tell me today's blood work came back and my white cell count is 1.9! To some people a .5 increase doesn't sound like much, but to me it is a cause to praise the Lord and thank my brothers and sisters in Christ. Prayers do make differences! Thank you precious people.

Many people told us they were praying for Bill. We were so grateful. Their prayers have made a difference.

God is so faithful in caring for Bill. He knows exactly what Bill will need as he faces each treatment. In August 2004, Bill wrote this e-mail:

> Just wanted to let you know that the treatment went very well today, and I feel fine. To the praise of our wonderful Father in the answering of prayer, especially last night at the Atlanta Bread Company when several of God's finest saints prayed for me, my blood count this morning was the highest it has ever been 8.8! I believe the Father wanted to build up my blood count in preparation for this series of treatments as they are the strongest I have received to date. Thanks, men, for "huddling" with me last night and for all of you who have been so faithful to ask the Lord's blessing on me. Barbara and I are truly humbled by the outpouring of so much love and support from all of you. We thank God for every expression of your kindness and prayers.

We have seen the evidence of the power of prayers over and over as God is accomplishing His work. Bill's immune system continues to be built up as a result of prayer, and our lives have a blessed infusion from God as a result of divine intervention.

The next series of treatments would keep Bill's cancer in check for six months. Bill wrote this e-mail to our friends.

> I met with my oncologist this morning to discuss the next round of treatments for my "inconvenience." He will start me on a new drug next Tuesday a.m. called Cytoxan, which is a more powerful chemo than I have taken to date. The treatment will last about two hours, and I will return the next day for an injection to assist my bone marrow in the development of blood cells. My understanding at this point is that I will have this treatment on Tuesday and then have another one three weeks later. The number of treatments is undetermined at this time and will depend upon obtaining the desired results. There are a number of side effects with this drug that I have not had with the others. I will continue to be very susceptible to infection and fatigue, and it is a given that I will lose my golden locks! I've considered shampooing with

Superglue, but then again, I look at Donn Harbin, a friend with little hair on his head, and I think, *That's not such a bad-looking guy!*

The Lord had much to teach me about His sufficiency and helping me to recognize my own smallness. The apostle Paul said in 2 Corinthians 3:5 (NKJV), "Not that we are sufficient of ourselves to think of anything as being from ourselves, but our sufficiency is from God." I'm so awed at how God works. He truly uses our circumstances for opportunities to show His power. God of the universe hears our prayers and answers accordingly to His divine purposes. My heart's prayer is, "That they may know that You alone, whose name is the LORD, are the Most High over all the earth" (Ps. 83:18).

When I sometimes feel I am going to the back side of a mountain, I need to recall that Moses found a burning bush on the back side on his mountain, and an encounter with Jehovah God that transformed his life. The unknown and uncertainties of this journey are not as worrisome to me as compared to the assurance of God's Word that He has ordered our steps and knows the end from the beginning of this journey. I have anchored my soul on a Rock that will not be moved, and like David "I will cry to God Most High, To God Who accomplishes all things for me" Psalm 57:2. Again, in Psalm 138:8 (NASB) David confidently says, "The Lord will accomplish what concerns me" and then as on a pillow he lays his human frailty on this comforting reminder, "Your lovingkindness, O LORD, is everlasting."

There may not be easy answers to the challenges Bill and I were facing, but I knew I didn't have to face the overwhelming challenges of life alone. God's people were faithfully praying for us. Prayers were indeed Divine channels through which the grace and power of the Father was flowing to us. I saw that truth firsthand as God was pouring out an overflow of loving-kindness upon Bill and me. God was working His plans. After all, He is the Master of the universe, and if He chooses, He could heal Bill regardless of the medical field's prognostics, "not curable." I have not seen Bill's cancer cure yet, but that did not stop me or others from praying for total healing and believing God for whatever He wanted to do. I prayed and others prayed because God tells us to pray, and He promises that He both hears and answers our prayers. I was seeing many examples of God's power of divine intervention causing me to embrace God's greatness.

CHAPTER 7

Learning to Give Thanks in Everything

Through all of these life circumstances, God wanted not only to see how I would trust Him with the unknown and the suffering but also to see how I would respond. Christians have situations just like everyone else, but the way we respond to those hardships and trials is what should distinguish us from non-Christians. I did not always do so well with my response. As you are reading through these chapters, you will see my struggles. I'm thankful God kept working in me, for He never gave up on me even during those days when I grappled with seeing the ultimately good plan and purposes God had for Bill and me.

I learned firsthand that giving thanks and rejoicing in everything can be hard especially when life dishes out cancer for someone you love. Life can appear to be so unfair. I know that to be true. Life did not seem fair to Habakkuk, yet the prophet's response to his situation brought rejoicing in the Lord.

> Though the fig tree does not bud
> and there are no grapes on the vines,
> though the olive crop fails
> and the fields produce no food,
> though there are no sheep in the pen
> and no cattle in the stalls,
> yet I will rejoice in the LORD,
> I will be joyful in God my Savior.
> The Sovereign LORD is my strength;
> he makes my feet like the feet of a deer,
> he enables me to go on to the heights. (3:17–19)

Considering the prophet probably depended on the fertility of his flocks and fields for his source of livelihood, his situation could not have gotten much worse. And yet, even in the midst of his own hardship, he still rejoiced in the Lord.

The Lord knew some lessons about rejoicing in Him and having a joyful attitude would benefit me. I needed to get over my attitude about life not being fair and embrace life with a joyful assurance that God is my strength and in Him is the joy that keeps me going even in the mist of difficult situations. I have a choice every day regarding my attitude, and one thing I cannot do is walk around with a long face. I cannot change the fact that Bill has cancer. I cannot change the inevitable that there may not be an assurance of a cure, but I can respond the way my Lord has instructed me. He has told me to rejoice in the Lord. A joy-filled life is God's will.

If you were to ask my three grown children, "What song do you recall your mother singing to you when you were a young child?" They would all agree it would be the song I sang each morning. It's based on Psalm 118: "This is the day, this is the day that the Lord has made, that the Lord has made, I will rejoice, I will rejoice and be glad in it." This is the song they remember as I flipped on their bedroom lights singing ecstatically. Our two boys shared a room with bunk beds next to our daughter's room. As they aroused from their night's sleep, I was clapping my hands, singing the song over and over, moving about the bedrooms until my children got slowly out of their beds. As preschoolers they loved this morning ritual and did not mind that mom could not carry a tune. However, by the time they reached their teenage years, their enthusiasm had waned. "Oh Mom, not again," they cried, pulling their blankets over their heads, hoping I would turn off the light and just go away. One son even requested I just buy him an alarm clock, and he started locking his bedroom door at night!

When the psalmist wrote, "This is the day the LORD has made; let us rejoice and be glad in it" (Ps. 118:24), I'm not sure just all he had in mind. Could it have been the day the temple was dedicated or maybe when God's children crossed the Red Sea? For many generations the Israelites made this psalm their own and counted their day as "the day the LORD has made." I wonder if the Israelite mothers woke their children singing this song. I can picture in my mind Jesus singing this psalm in perfect tune and harmony, for it became a part of the songs of triumph and thanksgiving Jews sang at their annual festivals, especially the Passover.

Over the years those words "the day the LORD has made" took on greater meaning, for they could apply to any day: the day of Christ's birth, the day the Savior became man; the day when Jesus died on the cross and paid the penalty for my sins; resurrection day, the day of days, when Christ demonstrated His power over death and the grave; the day of my conversion, like the day when God opened Lydia's heart, and I understood for the first time I am a great sinner and Christ is a great Savior. It will be the day of the coming again of our Lord, the day the trumpet will sound and time will be no more.

The day the Lord has made was the day I married my husband. It was the day I gave birth to our children. It is the days our grandchildren were born, seeing them take their first breath of life. It was the day we got the call every parent fears, "Your child has been in a car accident. The ambulance has just left." It was the day when Bill, my precious husband, was diagnosed with cancer. And, yes, it was the day my father died one month after we learned he had pancreatic cancer.

As a young mother, I wanted my children to learn that every day is made by God and is a gift from Him. I wanted them to be joyful no matter what disappointments they might face in life. They would have problems, but they could face them with optimism and hope. Having a positive attitude of rejoicing would enable them to get through many difficult challenges. Now, years later, the summer of 2004, those lessons about rejoicing are ones I need to remember and practice.

At the age of eighty-four, Dad had a clear mind. He could recall stories of what had taken place half a century earlier. Just two weeks earlier, he sat in his blue chair moving across time, sharing stories from the past. "When I was a young boy, I used to . . . ," he said as he laughed under his raspy, weak voice. I drew closer to hear every word, not wanting to miss anything. "Do you remember, Dad, when we went fishing and you lost your favorite hat while you were helping me bait my hook," I reminded Dad about that cold, windy afternoon. He smiled and nodded his head, "That was a long time ago." "Yes, it was, but it doesn't seem like it," I whispered as I touched his check. Dad's voice was not as strong, but his spirits were high.

As I sat beside my father's bed, holding his hand that July morning of 2004, my life flashed before me like images in a slideshow. I thought about my childhood and the good times we had shared. My dad has always been in my life, but now he was dying. The chart next to his bed read, "Very weak, lethargic, and unresponsive." I can't believe Dad's body is shutting down. I tuck another blanket around his long skinny frame because his feet are always cold now. For the past four days his hospice nurses have said, "Your dad won't make it through the day." He is so near death, but he keeps breathing, hanging on to the little life still left in his frail, yellow body.

So much had transpired these past weeks, and I tried to sort out what had happened. My dad had never been sick with anything major. Being the healthy one in the family, he took care of my mom who had ongoing health problems. In fact, my sister and I always thought mother would be the first to die because of her congestive heart condition and dementia. We had kidded mother about how we had picked out dad's next wife, one of the widow ladies from their Sunday school class. Mother sometimes did not find that as amusing as we did, but we all knew dad would have a hard time living by himself.

Dad's cancer diagnosis had shocked our family. After one week in the hospital, the doctors confirmed that nothing else can be done for him. His rapidly deteriorating condition meant death was certain. The cancer was more extensive than the doctors anticipated; it had spread throughout his body. The news was devastating. "Barbara, I'm going home to live out the rest of my life. I don't want to die in the hospital. I want to be home with my family," Dad said. I held the phone tightly, trying to keep my voice from breaking: "Dad, I'm coming home. I'll be there for you." Bill had just finished his treatments for the week so I felt comfortable about getting a flight out of Nashville that evening.

My father being at peace with the news he was dying, signed papers before he left the hospital to be under hospice care. Hospice is a program that provides special in-home care for people who are near the end of life. My sister and I quickly made some modifications to our parents' home in Irving, Texas. We made room for the necessary equipment the hospice professionals would need for Dad's care. Moving the king-size bed to the garage gave plenty of space for the hospice bed and a twin bed for Mom so she could be near Dad. We did not want the room to resemble a hospital environment so we brought matching twin bed sets and placed a beautiful stained glass angel picture in the bedroom window. We pulled out boxes of family photos and covered the walls with them. Mom and Dad's wedding picture hung in the middle surrounded by other family memories. Making this bedroom special was one way we could show our love for our dad and honor our mother as she would spend these last days with her husband of sixty-three years.

The medicine kept Dad free from pain. Although he was extremely weak, his mind remained sharp. We spent many hours reminiscing about the past. He gave instructions about Mom's care, making sure she would have all of her needs met. He told my sister, "I want you to make sure your mother has plenty of money in her purse, but don't give her big bills. Give her ones and fives because she handles that better."

Dad finalized some business transactions and even called the funeral director explaining their services would soon be needed. Dad made all the arrangements, selecting his casket and the suit and tie he would be buried in. He chose the hymns to be sung at his memorial service. Dad wanted Bill to preach if he was physically able. Having the service all planned, Dad asked my sister to bring him his checkbook, and with pen in hand he wrote a check to pay for his funeral expenses. He asked the funeral director, "Now, how much do I owe you? I want to pay for my wife's service also. Just add that cost to my bill. Is there a discount for two?" That was just like my father, wanting the most for his money as well as thinking about the future care of our mother.

Besides communicating clearly his last wishes, my father talked about his life. He had no fear of death, only concerns about leaving Mother. He knew he had a home in heaven, for he had taken care of that decision as a young man. His peace and trust were in Jesus Christ, and when visitors came to see him, he would tell them, "I'm going to be with Jesus real soon, and everything is going to be all right." Even in the bleakest times, my dad had the brightest hope.

The week with my father was truly a beautiful time. In spite of dealing with the reality of his impending death, I found joy in the midst of it. We spent many hours recalling the past, laughing and crying as Dad and I recaptured many memories. Everything was happening so fast. My emotions were torn with wanting to be in Texas with my father but also feeling the need to get back to Nashville for Bill. He would be starting another series of treatments the next week. It didn't feel right for me to leave Dad now, but it also didn't feel right for me not to be with Bill. Now both my father and Bill were living with cancer, and both had needs. There was simply not enough of me to go around. I cried out to God and tried to understand all that was happening. God used my dad to give me peace about what I should do. Dad said to me in his fatherly tone, "Now Barbara, you get back on that plane and go be with Bill. He needs you. I'm going to be fine." That's what I did.

About ten days later I drove to Texas with my daughter and her children. Our two boys joined us as we spent some days with Mom and Dad. I looked into my father's drawn face and saw the paleness of death across his sunken flesh. How could my father, whose joy of life could energize a group, be losing his fight to keep that life? I watched him struggle to walk. Everything he did appeared to be in slow motion.

Having some of his grandchildren and great-grandchildren visit with him appeared to boost his weakening body. I was so grateful Bill had encouraged me to go, for this was the last time I would see my father able to communicate and laugh. Just a few days later my sister called on a Saturday morning and said, "Dad woke up this morning, sat up in bed, and then just fell back. He is unable to talk or move."

I pulled all the blinds back letting the full sunshine steam across his face and propped Dad's head up with two pillows. His eyes were closed, and his arms lay flat against the sheet. I gently folded his arms across his chest. Dad's heavy breathing was now a murmuring sound. The music played in the background as I sang softly, caressing my father's hand. I kissed his forehead and whispered in his ear. "Dad, it's OK. You can go now. I love you."

My sister and I will always remember that last day with our father. We read Scripture verses, sang songs, prayed, and talked to Dad as if he could hear every word we uttered. We lovingly washed his arms and legs, put clean pajamas on his lifeless body, and wrapped him in clean sheets. I shaved the few whiskers on his chin and patted his favorite cologne around his face while my sister washed his dry mouth and rubbed smoothing lotion on his thin skin.

I was experiencing joy that day. Some people would say, "How can you rejoice and be glad during this deep and dark situation, watching your father die?" The answer is this: the Lord is my joy. "In Your presences is fullness of joy." Psalm 16:11. The Lord empowers me to be joyful no matter how dire my circumstances appear to be. "We are pressured in every way but not crushed; we are perplexed but not in despair," Paul stated in 2 Corinthians 4:8 (HCSB). Joy is not emotional ecstasy. It is the feeling deep inside knowing that with God's help the present and future will be alright even if it involves pain or the prospect of death.

I felt God touching my innermost being, giving me a restful contentment of trust as Dad breathed in and out, in and out, slowly taking his last peaceful breath. My earthly father entered into the everlasting arms and presence of his Heavenly Father. What blessed joy that is!

Many times I have heard, "A time to be born and a time to die" (Eccl. 3:2). My father had now experienced both birth and death. God's timing is always perfect even when I question it. I need not resist God's ways. The sovereign God orders everything for His own holy purposes. He is working all things after the counsel of His own will, making all things work together for good. Yes indeed, the times, the seasons, and the opportunities of life are controlled by a sovereign God. He controls life and death.

I have read all sorts of predictions of how long a person will live with certain kinds of cancers, but those are only educated guesses. I have heard some other people say that if you have cancer, you are on borrowed time. Cancer is not always an automatic death sentence. Some people like my dad may die quickly, but others will survive their disease.

Our times are ultimately in God's hands so I need not fear death or be so concerned about how long I will live. Being depressed, unhappy, and pessimistic is not the way I'm to respond to cancer and death. I love the apostle Paul's take on life and death, "To live is Christ and to die is gain" (Phil. 1:21). My father did not fear death. He saw it as gain. He lived each day to the fullest until he died. What an example he was for me!

This day I am alive. I will count it all joy and will choose to rejoice and be glad no matter what my circumstances might be. I will live each day as if it is the only day I have, for no one knows what tomorrow may bring, whether gain or loss, life or death. I have learned to live in the present. I don't know what tomorrow holds, but I know the Person who holds tomorrow, and I do not need to fear death. For me that is enough because I also know that in the midst of any difficult moments God can teach me to rejoice and be glad. Psalm 104:10 (HCSB) says, "He causes the springs to gush into the valleys; they flow between the mountains."

Nobody can take away what God has given me, His joy! I do not know what tomorrow will bring; cancer is so unpredictable. I do know that I can rejoice because my joy is in the Lord. "Shout joyfully to God, all the earth, Sing the glory of His name; Make His praise glorious." (Ps. 66:1–2).

This tribute to my father was written in November 2004:

> **God does not say to grieve not; instead, His word says, "But we do not want you to be uninformed, brethren, about those who are asleep, so that you will not grieve as do the rest who have no hope." (1 Thess. 4:13)**
>
> **"And I know that after this body has decayed, this body shall see God! Then he will be on my side! Yes, I shall see him, not as a stranger, but as a friend! What a glorious hope" (Job 19:26–27).**
>
> **November is a time for declaring loudly our expressions of thanksgiving. We are blessed when we express to one another and to our gracious heavenly Father the many things for which we are grateful. On my list is thankfulness for my earthly father, Kenneth L. Ford. I pay tribute to him and celebrate his life for all that he has meant to our family and to so many friends. He touched our lives and we will forever hold his memory dear to our hearts.**
>
> **Four months ago we said good-bye to him as he left this earth to join his Lord and Savior Jesus Christ. He had faith in his Lord, and the Scripture verse found in Hebrews 11:1 was a testimony of his life. "Faith is being sure of what we hope for and certain of what we do not see." This day he is seeing it all, and he is rejoicing and praising the God of heaven and earth who has given him life beyond this earth. I know if Dad could talk to you personally today, he would tell you of the great love for God and how important it is to have a personal relationship with Christ.**
>
> **Two Scripture passages bring great comfort. Ephesians 2:8, "It is by grace you have been saved, through faith—and this not from yourselves, it is the gift of God," and 1 John 5:4, "Everyone born of God overcomes the world. This is the victory that has overcome the world, even our faith."**

Dad would want his children, grandchildren, and great-grandchildren to experience God's love and grace. "Believe on the Lord Jesus Christ, and you will be saved" (Acts 16:31 NASB).

I continue to miss my dad, and at times my grief is great. However, the pain gradually lessens when I reflect on all the great promises of God. A special verse found in Philippians 1:21 discloses a great truth, "For to me, to live is Christ and to die is gain."

CHAPTER 8

God's Heavenly Sandpaper

The year 2004 was filled with a gambit of emotions, sending me reeling with feelings of helplessness and heartbrokenness. My heart had been wrung out so many times I was sure it was wrinkled. The apparent inability of sustaining the production of new white blood cells in Bill's bone marrow alarmed me, not to mention the other family concerns and events that became overwhelming. Bill's mom died in February. My Dad died in July. Our sister-in-law Frieda was battling brain cancer. She would die the following year. Why does cancer have such a nasty habit of taking things away from people—hair, appetite, a leg, and even a loved one?

These are difficult questions to answer. I had a hard time coming to terms with the fact God was allowing these kinds of adversity to come into my life. I experienced days when I wanted to go back to believing that cancer was something other families had to face. I frantically cried out, "Lord, get me out of these circumstances!" I found myself tangled in the web of adversity, and I wanted an escape route.

I love what someone shared with me several years ago. I recall it well. If a train goes through a tunnel and it gets dark, you don't throw away the ticket and jump off. You sit still and trust the engineer. That's great advice! I cannot change what has happened, nor can I go back and try to erase the day that cancer came into my family. When I am constantly looking back, or wanting this nightmare to end, I might just miss the meaningful moments of today. As I stand in the land of today, I will trust my Engineer as He guides this cancer through this dark tunnel wherever it might lead me or how it might take away my family or other parts about life.

I know God certainly has the power to stop bad things from happening, but sometimes He does not stop them. On the contrary, I think He allows me to go through those adversities for various reasons. I may never know for sure all the reasons until I meet Him face-to-face, but I do know that God is using adversities to do His work in my life. Adversities are like God's heavenly sandpaper, refinishing those areas in my life that definitely need some refining.

Life can be tough, and experiences can hurt, but the end results can be good as God uses those adversities for His divine purposes.

I'll never forget the day I brought my grandmother's antique dresser home to refinish. Because of fond memories of my grandparents and especially the old homestead farm where my father grew up, I eagerly received this piece of furniture that had been passed down from one generation to the next even though it was in awful shape. Its appearance was rather rough and needed a great deal of attention.

My paternal grandparents had lived for years on a farm outside of Gage, Oklahoma. When I was a young child, my family spent every Christmas with them. The farmhouse and its meager furnishings became a place where my aunts, uncles, and a houseful of cousins gathered to enjoy family time around a table filled with grandmother's fried chicken, homemade biscuits spread with fresh churned butter, and an assortment of vegetables Mama Ford had canned the previous summer and kept in her cellar. I still picture that cellar deep in the ground with its chill and musty smell. I have a permanent scar on my knee from falling down the cellar steps as I ran after my big brother one summer afternoon.

Mama Ford would get up early every morning to milk the cows. She even gave me a few lessons on milking, but I never could get the rhythm of pulling and squeezing. I remember pumping the water from an outside well and for several years using the outhouse located behind the barn. How delighted we all were on that first trip after my grandparents got indoor plumbing. No more having to go outside in the middle of winter. My grandparents were so proud of this modern convenience, and I was equally thrilled, especially since my brother loved to tell his little sis scary stories about creatures coming out of the hole.

My grandparents did not have a lot of earthly possessions, but I experienced so much love and joy while visiting them. I guess that's why now having this antique piece of furniture gave me a connection to my childhood past and the history it represented.

The dresser needed to be refinished after years of abuse and neglect. It had numerous scratches and nicks in the wood. The peeling paint revealed several coats of white and yellow, indicating past efforts to refurbish it. The piece was definitely unkempt, dull looking. So my first reaction after bringing it home was that maybe I didn't really need this in my home. After all, it looked like a piece of junk next to my newer furniture. "This is so ugly it belongs in my dark attic out of sight from everyone. Remove it," I said to my husband after reexamining its condition. It's not something I want in my house. The beauty in that old piece of furniture could no longer be seen by the human eye. However, my husband saw the potential. Together we sandpapered for days, removing the layers of paint and years of use. After several coats of varnish, that old antique dresser took on a fresh new glow of beauty. Today that dresser is in my living room. It is a beautiful, treasured, and useful piece of furniture.

My first response to cancer had been to try to remove it. I reacted to it with great fear. I didn't want this adversity to touch my family, for it appeared so ugly, destructive, and hurtful by the world's perspective, but God had other plans. God knew that the most devastating events in my life can actually be my greatest assets for God's purposes. He would use these trials to remove the dross from my life, for I needed a spiritual wake-up call to a new way of living. My husband's fight with cancer and all of the adversities I would experience during these years would clearly be the instruments to get me back on track. Affliction and adversities would become God's heavenly sandpaper, and He would use it in His heavenly workshop to transform something awful into a blessing from the Creator. God would use it to refine and reshape my life.

Sandpaper is useful and important in refinishing a rough and ugly looking plank of wood; likewise, God's heavenly sandpaper was needed to refinish some rough, ugly, fagged edges in my life. His loving hands with His carefully designed sandpaper would rub against my life conforming me into His likeness, renewing me into the image of Christ. Through these trials and testing, the Master Craftsman is taking me, His creation, and making me better fit for His services. He plans were to bring good things into my life through these adversities. He was remodeling my life.

I had no idea at the beginning how God would use every experience for my good and how the challenges we faced would profoundly impact my life and the lives of others, but God knew what He was doing. He continues to teach me much through these situations, so I don't need to waste my time looking for ways out or resist God's heavenly sandpapering. These trials are meant to have application, for they provide the classroom for my learning. I once heard someone say that the best classroom in the world is when you are facing an adversity. It becomes the training ground for my preparedness to serve. God can fine-tune me so I can be more compassionate, more caring, more loving, and more aware of others' pain. I can encourage others whose journey is just beginning that there is hope in Christ Jesus, and they, too, can survive their adversities.

My Mighty Lord does not make mistakes, for all things first must pass through His sovereign fingers. He knows how the sandpaper will define His grace and beauty in me. After much work from human hands, my grandmother's old antique dresser glows with a fresh shining finish. It now is an acceptable, beautiful, useful piece of furniture. My life is also going to be touched with fresh, glowing paint from my Heavenly Father's hand as He continues to renew a stronger spirit of faith in me that I pray shines through these adversities.

One of the first things God wanted to do in my life as He was working on my fresh glow was to humble me. My pride gauge indicated a self-sufficiency attitude that needed some overhauling. God was using Bill's cancer that would not go away to show me I was in His hands, and I could do nothing but trust Him with these adversities. God is all-sufficient. Without God's grace I am nothing. God also knew exactly where I needed to go to get what I needed to live through these experiences. My spiritual trek would take me right to the Bible.

I found such great consolation from the Holy Scriptures. God's Word strengthens me and helps me face the many challenges of living with and ministering to family members diagnosed with cancer. God's wonderful precious promises gave me hope and opened my heart to see God's power at work. I am so glad I can claim God's promises, for no matter what the future holds, I can always trust God's promises. His promises gave me positive answers during those times when I had so many questions about life. No matter what I was facing, God's presence stood strong. I leaned on Isaiah 43:2–3 (HCSB), "I will be with you when you pass through the waters. . . . When you walk through the fire, . . . the flame will not burn you. For I [am[the Lord your God, the Holy One of Israel, and your Savior."

When I saw my father die, Jesus said, "I have prepared for him a better place" (see John 14:1–4). When I see no cure for Bill, Jesus said, "All things are possible" (Matt. 19:26). When I don't see how I can get through another day, God says, "My grace is sufficient for you, for My strength is made perfect in weakness" (2 Cor. 12:9). God does not always take away the problem. Instead He gives the grace to live with it. When I don't see how we can pay all the medical bills, God says that He will take care of my needs, When I'm afraid Bill will die, God says, "I have not given you a spirit of fear" (see 2 Tim. 1:7). When I worry about how Bill will respond to the next chemo treatment, God says, "Cast all your cares on Me" (see Ps. 55:22). When I'm tired from sleepless nights, Jesus says, "I will give you rest" (Matt. 11:28). When I can't fix this cancer problem and can't figure life out, God says that He will direct my steps.

Spending time with the Lord gave me the strength I needed while I cared for Dad and watched him die. I leaned on God for support. As a caregiver, I sometimes needed to rest not only my body but also my soul. Resting in God's Scriptures and knowing He was with me during dad's death gave me peace. No matter how dark it got in those difficult experiences, God gave hope, and His directions enabled me to survive those circumstances.

As I witnessed and personally felt the effects of each of those difficult situations during 2004, God's promises and truths became steadfast for me. He gave back in spite of the challenges by equipping me with what I needed to get through each of those adversities. The Word became a fruit-bearing tree from which I harvested nourishing produce, allowing me to taste of the Lord and to know He is good (see Ps. 34:8). Scripture verses became more alive and meaningful. The Word of God energized my life. I knew the truth of 1 Corinthians 2:9: "No eye has seen, no ear has heard, no mind has conceived what God has prepared for those who love Him" and of Jeremiah 15:16: "When your words came, I ate them; they were my joy and my heart's delight." The Bible is the living, powerful Word of God in which I encountered the Lord and discovered how to live in my situation and honor Him.

I am thankful God put this new thirst in me that could only be satisfied through an encounter with the Holy One. I had an insatiable desire to keep reading the Bible. I knew that if I would seek Him, His Word tells me I will find Him. More than ever I wanted to have a quiet time, sitting in His presence and listening to what He wanted to say to me.

God used His Written Word, the Bible, to speak to me timely messages that have given me encouragement and hope during those difficult years. I especially found great insights from the Psalms as the psalmist's words enriched my heart. Those passages kept my focus on the Shepherd of Israel who loves His sheep and bears them on His strong shoulders. My heart was also refreshed from the study of Joseph from the book of Genesis. God's eternal plan and His daily faithfulness as seen in the life of Joseph helped me have the peace and strength I needed as I cared for Bill.

I found a great example of how sufferings and illness is often the vehicle God uses to deliver His blessings from the Old Testament story of Job. Job had experienced a string of hardships that seemed to come for no reason. Like Job, my challenges and crisis were taxing me to the very end of my strength and during those moments it became easy to want to just give up. However, in the story of Job, I found encouragement and it gave me the power to persevere during my darkest hour. Job didn't understand why all of these events were happening in his life. Even though things did not make sense to him, Job trusted God.

It still is a mystery to me why bad things seen to happen for no apparent reasons. Life is full of many hurtful things as well as many blessing. I know God has a plan whether it makes sense to me. Rather than asking the why questions, I needed to be asking, what can I learn from this experience, and what can I do to help others for God's glory? Many blessings do come from trusting God during those times of adversities.

The Lord was giving wisdom, knowledge and understanding as I read His Word. He became a shield for me, guarding my path and preserving my way. God was changing me through His Holy Scripture. Many rich treasures of God's truth were waiting to be discovered. I'm amazed also at how God has used people and their writings to encourage me. I read many things Bill wrote as he worked through his own emotions to understand God's plans. He would affix notes and Scripture verses to his desk claiming the promises found in God's Word. I loved reading what he wrote; and when we moved to a different house, I packed all of those notes away, wanting to cherish those encouraging words. I want to share a few of those with you because they blessed my life.

When I have done all I can, then all I can is done. After all I can do is done is when God is free to do all He can do, and all He can do is more than all I need.

My thought process is most impressive when I base it on correct assumptions.

My happiness is not based on circumstances but on the faithfulness of God.

He will call upon me, and I will answer him; I will be with him in trouble, I will deliver him and honor him (Ps. 91:15).

God has caused me to be fruitful in the land of my affliction (Gen. 41:52 NKJV).

You can waste time, but you cannot squander (conserve) it. You can spend time, but you cannot hoard (buy) it; you can give time but you cannot keep it. So just use it wisely.

Age and death are the unavoidable consequences of birth.

Cast you cares on the LORD and he will sustain you; he will never let the righteous fall (Ps. 55:22).

I will cry out to God Most High, to God who performs all things [fulfills His purpose] for me (Ps. 57:2).

The LORD will perfect (fulfill His purpose for me) that which concerns me (Ps. 138:8 NKJV).

I will meditate on the glorious splendor of Your majesty, and on Your wondrous works (Ps. 145:5 NKJV).

Therefore, those also who suffer according to the will of God shall entrust their souls to a faithful Creator in doing what is right (1 Pet. 4:19 NAB).

"For I know the plans [thoughts] that I have for you," declares the LORD, "plans for welfare [peace] and not for calamity to give you a future and a hope. Then you will call upon Me and come and pray to Me, and I will listen to you" (Jer. 29:11). This is the verse that Bill and I claimed from the very start of our journey with cancer.

When I'm going through adversities, I have to remind myself that God's eye is on me at all times, and He cares for me and understands my feelings even when I don't understand them. He is my constant Friend. I love to hear one of my favorite gospel singers, George Beverly Shea, sing, "His Eye Is on the Sparrow," for it puts so much of life into perspective. Jesus is watching over me, and His love will see me through all of my trials.

All of the trials and adversities I go through definitely have the Father's eternal purposes on them as they are tailored to His specific plan for my life. Life situations, including afflictions, are becoming my instructors to train me in the art of walking by faith not by sight, knowing that the Governor of heaven "works all things according to the counsel of His will" (Eph. 1:11 NKJV). With renewing faith I believe God can do the impossible and my covenant-keeping God does not go back on His promises. He will not fail me; He loves me in the midst of all of this chaos and pain.

Life is a series of trials, and in the summer of 2006, I would face an adversity that would either make me or break me. Once again my faith would be tested to the limit. You will see as you read the next chapters what I did with this new adversity and how I felt when Bill's oncologist said, "Bill, I know you have always considered this cancer just an inconvenience, but now it is more than that. This is not good. We are running out of options." The devastating news about Bill's deteriorating health would take me to a deep dark pit, and I wasn't sure how to get out of it. My life appeared to be falling apart, and I was having difficulty understanding. I certainly did not see any good coming out of the distressing report. With the reality of Bill's deteriorating health in front of me, I felt so helpless. I did not know what the outcome would be, nor did I understand this difficult period in my life. My faith would really be tested as I witnessed the truth of these words "The flame shall not harm thee; I only design thy dross to consume and thy gold to refine." God's purpose will always go beyond the pit.

CHAPTER 9

When Life Takes You to a Pit

I sit on the edge of the hospital bed that October night of 2006, rubbing my husband's back while he lies on his side with his knees pulled up close to his chest. He has found a comfortable position. My eyes focus on his frail face. Propped against some pillows, he looks so thin, pale, and fatigued. The treatments are taking their toll. Scattered on his pillow are clumps of hair that have continued to fall out. I put a cold, wet washcloth on his forehead and keep the vomit pan close by. The round clock directly in front of the bed tells the time. It is 3:00 a.m. Will morning ever come? The light coming from the bathroom gives the only sign of a hope for daybreak. The blind over the solitary window is close, keeping out the Nashville city lights.

My life has been brought to a standstill waiting for this to be over. The five days of heavy doses of various chemo therapies and fluids flowing continuously into Bill's veins has turned into three weeks. Originally the treatment protocol, five days in the hospital and then two weeks off, would then repeat itself with another round of the five-day treatments. These series were designed to attack the cancerous lymphoma aggressively, and if a response is achieved, Bill will proceed with the stem-cell transplantation. The first series has not gone as planned. On the third day Bill developed a fever with chills along with nausea, vomiting, abdominal pain, and diarrhea. His consistent cough keeps him with a shortness of breath even though his lungs appear to be clear.

Tears roll down my cheeks, sometimes just a trickle and sometimes turning into heavy sobs, desperately crying for healing. I feel so helpless wanting Bill to be better. Bill's cancer has relapsed. I cry out to God. Why, God, is this happening again? When I look at Bill, I can see his once strong healthy body now becoming weaker as the pounds drops from his frame.

That fall, Bill was hospitalized the first time from October 23 to November 10. The second time was over the Thanksgiving holidays from November 20 to 27. Not only would most of this year's holidays be spent in a hospital room, but the year would prove to be the most challenging, heart-wrenching months of our lives. God took us to a deep pit. My emotions would range from closeness to God all the way down to the feelings of despair and gloom. I knew the triumphs on the mountain, but now at times I was experiencing in this pit a valley of despair feeling discouragement, isolation, hopelessness, and even some depression.

Bill's doctor of eight years had exhausted all treatment options. He said at one office visit, "Come back next week. I'm going to scratch my head and see what I can come up with." I was not ready for Bill to leave this world.

I felt so helpless. Cancer had become a deep dark pit, and as the months past during that year of 2006, I hit the bottom. This destructive pit appeared to have no way out. It was a nightmare. But God did something amazing! He climbed down in the pit with Bill and me, and He poured out His love until it was so much that it lifted us right out of the abyss. The healing touch of God became deeper than the pit. "Fear not, for I am with you; be not dismayed, for I am your God. I will strengthen you, yes, I will help you, I will uphold you with My righteous right hand" (Isa. 41:10 NKJV).

Our situation did feel like a deep pit, but the loving presence of God was deeper. My troubles would remind me to walk by faith and not by sight. I knew in my heart the love of God is deeper than any pit, including these new circumstances. I would see as the year ended that the purposes of God always goes beyond the pit, for the grace of God will always be sufficient. I claimed Psalm 27:13 (NKJV): "I would have lost heart, unless I had believed that I would see the goodness of the LORD in the land of the living." In the darkest pit of despair, when God gave me only the light to take one step at a time, His love message to me was once again, "Trust Me."

The year had started out with a great deal of excitement. In January Bill's health appeared to have turned around. No visible sign of cancer. It had been eighteen months since his last treatment which was Zevalin, a monoclonal antibody. This radioisotope procedure delivered radiation directly to cancer cells while sparing healthy tissue. So far this had been the most effective treatment achieving a response that actually lasted longer than any other treatment he had had.

Bill's physical energy matched his spirit. It was at an all-time high. Bill wrote this note in the church's newsletter:

Turning the corner on 2006 thrusts us into a new year/era of our lives. The old has gone. The new has come! We can only change habits and lifestyles, make fresh surrenders with new passions for holiness and spiritual growth. The gift and purpose of the Christ child should motivate us to seek first the kingdom of God and His righteousness. His banner over us is love. Let us

fly that ensign high in 2006 that those around us will know we are not ashamed of the gospel of Christ. For the glory of our Lord Christ, in whom grace abounds more and more.

In February I noticed some of Bill's lymph nodes beginning to enlarge, especially the ones under his arm. Something was happening. Bill's doctor put him on a high-dose prednisone. His nodes improved to some extent with the steroids. However, as the summer approached, one lymph node under Bill's arm became the size of a grapefruit, other lymph nodes were rapidly expanding. Something was wrong. This time the slow-growing cancer had picked up speed, and the cells were growing way too fast, sapping Bill's energy.

I would ask Bill, "How do you feel?" He would say, "I'm tired." After hearing those words for several weeks and observing his constant cough, I knew his health was declining. Even with afternoon naps he didn't have the stamina to finish a day's work. Bill kept pushing, trying to maintain the pastoral ministries at our church.

We had just completed our tenth month as pastor and wife of First Baptist Church in Lawrenceburg, Tennessee. The excitement about being in this new ministry kept us from the reality that something was terribly wrong with Bill's immune system. We were in denial. This couldn't be happening now, for we had just begun the work here. Bill kept preaching two services on Sunday plus leading a Wednesday evening Bible study; however, his energy level began to dwindle. The lymph nodes around his neck were visibly enlarging to the point that Bill had to buy new shirts. This sleeping cancer had decided to make itself known once again.

Life's sort of funny that way! At the moment when everything seems to be going smoothly, something happens to take us down a bumpy road and turns our life upside down. It is like the Bible story about the Israelite children. One moment they were surrounded by the palm trees, enjoying the grapes of Canaan, and drinking deep from the wells of Elim. Suddenly those grapes turned sour, and the water became bitter.

I once heard someone say that life is like a batter in a baseball game. About the time you think the next pitch is going to be a fastball, the pitcher throws a curveball. We were beginning to experience some curveballs. We were enjoying the good life, but now the bottom appeared to be dropping out.

Bill's white and red blood counts were plummeting. His oncologist scheduled a bone aspiration. After reviewing the test results, his oncologist said, "Bill, your bone marrow is full of weeds." We knew what the word "weeds" implied. The cancer had infested Bill's bone marrow and was doing havoc on the rest of his body.

In early June, Bill's oncologist consulted a specialist to investigate the possibility of a clinical study treatment. Since his blood levels were out of range, he did not qualify for any new protocol. "Next week, I want to start you on chemo treatments. I want to see what kind of response we get from the drug combination I'm going to put together for you," Bill's doctor said. Bill replied, "I can't do it next week because Barbara and I have scheduled a week's vacation in Williamsburg, Virginia."

The doctor gave Bill a somber look and said, "Bill, you are a very sick man, and I know you have always thought this cancer to be just a little inconvenience, but now this is serious." The doctor reluctantly agreed to reschedule the treatments; however, before we left the hospital, Bill received another blood transfusion.

The week in Virginia truly became an oasis of rest for both of us. Bill took naps throughout the days as we lounged around the condo. Just walking seemed to drain Bill, so we did a lot of reading and sharing. Truthfully, we remember this time as one of our most relaxing vacations. I believe we needed this getaway to prepare us for all we would face in the months to come. Cancer can affect all the family members, especially a spouse, so this time together gave us opportunities to release our fears and worries and talk about our future.

We discussed spiritual truths about God's providence. Bill shared this statement with me: "Providence is more of a diary than a road map." Looking back on my diary, I saw the benefits that had come from painful experiences. I found great hope when I rested in the fact that God would continue to uphold me no matter what I would encounter in the future. God's plans would come to pass.

The chemo started the week we returned home. Bill had always tolerated the chemo in the past, but this time he had a major reaction. He fainted about halfway through the first series of treatments. I watched as his eyes rolled back. His head dropped to his chest, and he slumped down into a lifeless position. I frantically called: "I need help! Someone please help my husband."

The nurses and doctor responded quickly, giving him oxygen. It was a scary moment. The chemo was stopped for the day. They took Bill to a private room, and the nurses monitored Bill over the next couple of hours. I had never seen Bill react to the chemo like this. It frightened me. This was not a good sign.

The next day our plans were to drive back to Nashville to finish the treatment. Afterwards we would go out for dinner to celebrate Bill's birthday.

The doctor had assured us the treatment would go much better this time. He would be adjusting the flow of the chemo, but that did not ease my apprehension about these drugs.

Before the procedure the routine required the nurse to check Bill's blood counts. The blood report indicated Bill's red counts as well as his platelets were at a critical level. So the doctor immediately cancelled the treatments and admitted Bill into the hospital for blood transfusions. If all went well, we were told that after the transfusions Bill could go home around 4:00 p.m. I was somewhat relieved Bill did not have to finish this round of chemo treatment, but my concerns about Bill's health had intensified.

As the day progressed, it became obvious we would not be out of the hospital by dinnertime. There had been a mix up in getting the transfusions from the blood bank. Wanting to make Bill's birthday special in spite of the unexpected circumstances, I went to the hospital gift shop to purchase some birthday goodies to help us celebrate. I bought ice cream sandwiches, chocolate moon pies, and a large singing balloon with *Happy Birthday* written in bold colorful letters. I loved this balloon because it played "Happy Birthday" in an upbeat western tune. I thought the music would certainly cheer up the hospital room. With only the slightest tapping of the balloon, it would play the song three times before it stopped.

I attached the balloon to the foot of Bill's bed, tapping it occasionally to remind my husband that today we were celebrating his birthday. For the first few times the song played, we both laughed and enjoyed it. After awhile the humor left. I didn't have to tap it for it to play. The balloon would start singing "Happy Birthday" at the slightest movement of air, especially when the nurses opened the door.

Other hospital staff came to our room and said, "I heard it's your birthday, Mr. Betts." The song could be heard in the hallways. The singing balloon got downright annoying as it continuously played the song over and over at the slightest movement. I tried to keep the balloon still so it wouldn't play. I could not stop it!

The last transfusion was completed around 1:45 the next morning. It had been a long night, but Bill still wanted to head for home even though it was late. Bill signed the release papers, and a nurse brought in a wheelchair to take Bill to the main lobby where a security guard would take us to our car.

Now picture this. Bill was seated in his wheelchair with a nurse pushing him. I followed toting the balloon. As I walked quietly down the hallway of this cancer floor, the balloon began to play "Happy Birthday." I gripped the top of the balloon string, hoping this will make it stop. Other patients were sleeping so I was walking fast trying to get to the elevator. Nevertheless, as I moved the song kept playing over and over.

At last we made it to the elevator. Quickly I made my escape to the far corner of the elevator. The song stopped, and we rode in silence. When we reached the first floor, the elevator bumped to a stop, and the song began to play as we made our grand exit. *How many times will it keep playing? Surely, it must be running out of juice by now.* I thought. The hospital security guard helped us into his vehicle, Bill in the front seat, while the balloon and I rode in the backseat.

Every time we went over a speed bump in the parking garage, the balloon started up again. The serious security guard tried to hide his laughter. By the time we got to our car, we had decided the best place for this balloon would be in the trunk. During the hour and half drive back to our home, the balloon continued to sing!

When we arrived home, I put the balloon in our spare bedroom and shut the door. The next day I gave it to our grandchildren, and their parents said it continued to play for a week. When Bill returned to the hospital in October, the nurses remembered us as the couple with the singing birthday balloon!

During those summer months Bill finished three series of treatments. Besides being nauseated, Bill experienced chills and fever. His body would go into uncontrollable shakes as the chemo dripped into his veins. The nurses would give him shots to counteract the tremors. I thought, *How much more can his body take?*

The fourth series had been scheduled for August 22, but instead of a treatment we met with the oncologist. In an ominous tone the doctor said, "Bill, the treatments are not working. You have a resistant disease, and now the cancer is not responding to the chemo." My head began to spin as he continued, "I told you from the beginning this cancer would be treatable not curable."

This devastating news gripped me, and I struggled to breathe. I felt the knots enthralling my stomach, and I swallowed the sobs I felt rising in my throat. I wanted to collapse against something strong to hold me as my hopes for a longer life with Bill were suddenly plummeting. I needed support. I asked the doctor, "What about a stem-cell transplant?" He replied, "That's not an option now. Bill is not a candidate for a bone-marrow transplant." Our oncologist had just informed us that in his opinion there was not much more he could do for Bill. I could scarcely believe what was happening. I felt like he was telling us to go home and get our affairs in order.

My heart began a raucous pounding in my chest, as I tried to pray. Nothing seemed to be working. I was not prepared for this. I felt an incredible letdown. My emotions revealed my hurt. I had so many questions. "God, I do not like this pit You have put me in. What do I do now?"

CHAPTER 10

Hope Finds Its Way out of the Pit

The day Bill's oncologist told us the devastating news that all standard procedures were exhausted, my hopes were dashed. This was the deepest pit I had ever experienced. I wanted to dig out of the dark, ditchlike dungeon; however, I couldn't even see how to climb out of it. The crater walls were collapsing, leaving me crushed, gasping for air. I desperately wanted out!

Time was running out for Bill. His body required more blood transfusions. Even his immune system, like my hope for Bill's recovery, was dwindling. Fighting off a common cold would be hard due to his low white blood counts. The struggle to maintain Bill's blood levels appeared to be losing ground. Bill's health and my state of mind had hit bottom.

Recalling a word coming from a farmer would be good advice for me now. "If you find yourself in a hole, the first thing to do is stop digging!" So from the trenches I cried out to God. My honesty with God, I believe, helped me take those first steps toward emotional and spiritual healing. As I took all of those difficult questions to God, I moved closer to the only One who truly has all the answers.

I refused to give up hope. I knew in my heart the love of God is deeper than any pit, and that my hope was anchored in the grace of God. "For in hope we have been saved, but hope that is seen is not hope; for who hopes for what he already sees? But if we hope for what we do not see, with perseverance we wait eagerly for it." Romans 8:24-25. Let me hold fast the confession of my hope without wavering for God is faithful. My God was with me in this unpleasant pit, and He was good at overcoming overwhelming odds. Psalm 34:18 (HCSB) confirms that promise. "The Lord is near the brokenhearted; He saves those crushed in spirit." My belief in God's Word became the sustaining power during this pit experience.

Isn't it just like God to do His greatest work when I find myself at my lowest point? That is when God takes over and begins working a miracle. In dark pits of despair, God gives me the light to take one step at a time. His message to me was once again simply, "Trust Me." If I ever doubt what God can do, I just need to look at Ephesians 3:20 (HCSB): "Now to Him who is able to do above and beyond all that we ask or think—according to the power that works in you." Nothing is too difficult for my Lord. I was going to see God do some amazing things.

A member of our church told Bill, "Pastor, you need to go to M. D. Anderson Cancer Center in Houston, Texas. It is recognized as the number one cancer center in the nation." Bill and I did some research on their Web site that evening and discovered it normally takes several months just to get an initial appointment; however, in less than two weeks we were notified to travel to Houston for an initial interview with doctors. We immediately arranged to send Bill's medical records to Texas.

On October 8, 2006, Bill and I flew to Houston for a weeklong evaluation at M. D. Anderson. Bill underwent a complete assessment of his health, including another bone-marrow biopsy, echocardiogram, pulmonary function test, MRI, chest x-ray, eye exam, dental exam, and daily blood test. He had more test this week than he had ever had in any one week. Besides meeting with a team of excellent doctors, we visited with a social worker, a patient advocate, plus staff from the business center. Bill and I carried a map of the facility as we trekked through the various hospital floors finding the right locale for our appointments.

After reviewing Bill's medical records from the past years and completing the initial examination, a doctor from the Department of Lymphoma/Myeloma said, "Bill, I think you need a stem-cell transplant, and I want to see if I can get you an appointment today in the Blood and Marrow Transplant Clinic."

The team at M. D. Anderson quickly determined one option for Bill would be a stem-cell transplant even though Bill's Nashville oncologist felt differently. As we left the examination room, walking down the hall toward the waiting room, Bill turned to me and said, "Isn't that interesting. One doctor says a transplant is not an option, but now it may be my best alternative."

Many questions ran through my mind as we made our way to the transplant clinic located on the eighth floor of the hospital. Just one hour after our initial consultation, the escalator door opened to a large waiting room. I scanned the room. Immediately I saw patients with masks covering their mouths seated in various, isolated parts of the room. I learned later that the people sitting next to the patients were usually their caregivers.

My eyes were drawn to the corner of the room where a large puzzle had been placed on a table. Two people sat putting pieces of the puzzle together. They were totally absorbed in working the puzzle. I had already noticed throughout the hospital, tables with unfinished puzzles were placed in various sections of the hospital floors. I thought, *What a neat concept, giving people something to do while they wait and perhaps helping distract them from the worries and frustrations of having cancer.*

Later as I reflected on the puzzles, I came up with another analogy. The puzzle represents the process involved in the treatment of cancer. It will require one step, one treatment, or one question answered at a time, putting each piece carefully in place. As the medical teams work together, just like many people will work on the puzzle, in time the picture will be complete. A life can be restored. All the treatments and medical procedures symbolize the many puzzle pieces. When the pieces are put together, it is a picture of health just like a completed puzzle picture.

I visualized how Bill's puzzle might come together. At that point the pieces were scattered on the table, but in time each piece will be put in the right place. The picture will be clearer as the process unfolds. I think the puzzle symbolized hope. A broken body can be put back together.

"What is involved in a transplant?" I asked the bone marrow transplant (BMT) doctor. He replied: "It is a procedure where healthy, normal, blood-forming cells are infused into a person. A transplant is needed when the bone marrow has been damaged or destroyed by disease, chemotherapy, or radiation." I thought, *Chemotherapy and cancer have certainly taken a toll on Bill's bone marrow. He does need some healthy blood cells, plus an overhaul in his bone marrow.*

The doctor continued to explain how the donor stem cells would graft into Bill's bone marrow, which is the spongy tissue found inside the cavities of large bones. If the transplant is successful, these new cells will begin to grow and produce new healthy cells that will eventually develop into mature tissues. As these cells divide, they make up the new blood and immune system— white cells that fight infection, red cells that carry oxygen and platelets that prevent bleeding. Without these healthy cells the immune system is severely impaired.

From our assigned transplant coordinator, we learned that a transplant patient will usually undergo chemotherapy and/or radiation to destroy their cancer and the diseased blood-forming cells. These treatments also suppress the immune system and act to prevent rejection from the transplant.

It could be a very risky procedure, but for Bill it might be the only medical hope for remission. When I read a pamphlet about the process, my reservations were many, especially when it explained that the preparation process could require lethal doses of chemotherapy intravenously and radiation. The sentence about the patient being "rescued" from death with a transfusion from a donor's healthy stem cells really alarmed me. In the past patients who were close to Bill's age were considered too old or perhaps too advanced in their disease to undergo a stem-cell transplant; nevertheless, many patients did try the risky procedure because they didn't have much to lose.

Patients in their mid-thirties or younger were considered better candidates because doctors believe they have a better chance of surviving the precarious procedure. But now, thank God, because of the improvements in the preparative regimens and less intensive chemotherapy before receiving a stem-cell infusion, many older patients like Bill are having successful transplants. I am counting not only on the divine intervention of my Heavenly Father, but on all of the knowledge and skill of the medical profession.

A door of hope gave me my first glimpse of light from the pit. We returned to Tennessee with the encouraging report in spite of the possibility that the grueling four- to five-month process may not work. M. D. Anderson's doctors designed an aggressive regimen of treatments to reduce the cancer in Bill's lymph nodes. These combinations of drugs had never been used on Bill in this particular format. I was encouraged about the possible outcome.

Bill's Nashville oncologist agreed to follow the treatment protocol so that Bill could have these treatments locally. The previous chapter gave you some insight about those weeks in the hospital, but what I did not tell was the amazing miracle. Bill's grapefruit size lymph nodes under his armpits as well as the ones in his neck area all reduced in size. The visible signs of enlarged lymph nodes disappeared. Bill's head was totally bald, but his cancerous nodes had shrunk. Bill had no outward signs of enlarged nodes.

The next miracle showed the magnitude of God's power. The hospital needed $263,000 for the cost of the stem-cell transplant. Bill's insurance coverage would only be $250,000. We needed to come up with $13,000 out of pocket before the hospital approved the transplant procedure. Our small nest egg in the bank was not near enough to cover the $13,000. I was ready to raise the money, sell something—maybe my diamond ring—borrow money, or ask for contributions or whatever sacrifices I could make. I'd do anything to make certain Bill got the medical care he needed.

Remember, I'm a fixer. However, Bill said, "We are not going to let anyone know about our need. We are going to ask God to take care of this little detail." Keeping our need a secret and bringing it only to the throne of God is what Bill did. He prayed, "God, help us to have the money to pay the hospital. We trust You with this need."

As the days past, the insurance company assigned a caseworker as an advocate for Bill. The transplant would not be approved by the hospital finance department until they had received from us the $13,000 payment. Right before the deadline to let the hospital know we could pay the $13,000, we received a call from the insurance case manager.

"Mr. Betts," she said, "You will not believe this. Are you sitting down?" Bill immediate thought the insurance company had worked out a deal with the hospital. The case manager continued, "We have never had this happen before, but as of November 1, 2006, the insurance company has increased its amount for stem-cell transplants from $250,000 to $1 million!" Now isn't that just like our God to do exceedingly abundant above all we ask or think. The Lord took care of that $13,000. One million dollars is but pocket change for my God, for everything belongs to Him.

God's love is deeper than any pit. The dungeons and roadblocks are only opportunities for God to transform pit ordeals into blessings. What am I to do with blessings? Give thanks. It is good to give thanks to the Lord. To give thanks to Jehovah is but a small return for the great benefits He blesses me with every day. Each day He loads me with benefits and blessings even while I am in a pit. "Blessed be the Lord, who daily loads us with benefits" (Ps. 68:19 NKJV). Not because I deserve them but because He is a benevolent Father and because He delights in showering His love upon His children. God gives me life, and I am admonished to give thanks in everything including pit experiences for this is the will of God in Christ Jesus concerning me.

What a blessing I experienced as I watched God take care of the needs Bill and I had. The cost of the transplant was just one of many testimonies of God's faithfulness and goodness to us. It is recorded in Jeremiah 29:11 (NKJV), "For I know the thoughts that I think toward you, says the LORD, thoughts of peace and not of evil, to give you a future and a hope." My pit ordeals were designed to accomplish God's plans to give me a future and a hope. I'm a different person as a result of my pit experiences.

During the stem-cell-transplant process and the months that would follow, I chronicled the journey with periodic newsletters to family and friends. As you read the rest of my story, you'll find those eighteen newsletters. The newsletters became a way to organize my thoughts, and sort out my feelings as I communicated with loved ones. You will see how God walked me through this journey as my husband's caregiver. He sometimes carried me but always lovingly showed His faithfulness during what I have called my "journey of faith." God gave light to the pathway out of my pit, and I will forever be thankful for what He taught me along the way.

Journey of Faith

November 28, 2006

We are moving closer to the date of the blood and stem-cell transplant and our stay in Houston, Texas. We have faith that Bill's cancer will be

eliminated through this process and that his health will be restored. When we first learned that this is the journey we must take, we felt overwhelmed and somewhat frightened by the unknown. However, as we have stepped out in faith, God has given us a peace and assurance that His loving hands and fingerprints are all over this journey. We are discovering anew that our Lord Jesus faithfully provides in even the smallest of details that affect our lives, and He sovereignly controls the events. We praise Him for what He is doing in our lives!

From the first contact with M. D. Anderson Cancer Center in October, we have felt that this is the place where Bill needed to go to receive the type of care required to address his cancer. The Transplant Center does more than six hundred transplants per year and maintains an integrated quality program in patient care, research, education, and prevention in a caring environment. We do not have the exact date of the transplant yet but expect that it will take place in late December. It is possible that we will have Christmas in Houston. Bill's brother, Bruce, is his donor match and is scheduled to be in Houston on December 13. He will be at M. D. Anderson as an outpatient for seven to ten days. At the end of that period, his stem cells will be collected (harvested) from his blood and frozen until Bill is prepared for the transplant.

Bill's preparation has already begun. He started a weeklong chemotherapy treatment regiment October 23 at Baptist Hospital in Nashville. That week's treatment turned into almost three weeks of hospitalization due to an infection and a suppressed immune system. We had a full week back at home with our church family, and then Bill returned to the hospital for another week of chemo on November 20. We spent Thanksgiving week in the hospital but were able to leave at the end of the week's stay.

Bill will be able to preach the Sundays of December 3 and 10 and then will return to Houston on December 11 for more testing and sessions with doctors in the Leukemia/Lymphoma Center. We hope to know about the transplant schedule in the next two weeks. Bill could possibly be admitted to the hospital that week, or he may get to come home for a couple of Sundays before we leave for the long stay. The total time we could be in Houston might be four to five months depending on how Bill responds to the transplant. For one month he could be in isolation, and the other months we will be living in an apartment near the Transplant Center making daily trips to the care center for follow-up and assessments.

Right before the transplant Bill will undergo more chemotherapy and/or radiation to destroy any remaining cancer and blood-forming cells. This treatment also suppresses the immune system and acts to prevent rejection of the transplant. He will be in a special unit called Protective Environment, where he will stay during the critical stage of the transplant. Healthy marrow/stem cells are then introduced into Bill's bloodstream. Then the bone marrow goes into the cavities of the large bones where it begins to grow (engrafts) and begins to produce new cells. Isn't it amazing what God has enabled the medical field to know and do!

During these next few weeks, we are busy with the numerous tasks that must be done in anticipation of being away from our home and work. Barbara will be taking a leave of absence from her job to be Bill's caregiver. M. D. Anderson requires a caregiver to be available twenty-four hours a day, seven days a week, to give support in the healing progress. Barbara will be with her husband throughout this entire journey and will count it a joy to be that daily encourager and supporter.

Our newsletter will give our church family and others a progress update of Bill's recovery and specific prayer requests. Already we have experienced the power of prayer and are grateful for so many prayer warriors. Will you begin praying with us for the following:

Pray that Bill's immune system will accept the transplant. (One of the potential complications is the Graft-Versus-Host disease. This occurs when the new bone marrow (the Graft) recognizes the tissues of the patient's body (the Host) as foreign and reacts against the body. There are two forms of Graft-Versus-Host Disease: acute (short-term) and chronic (long-term). Pray that Bill will not have either of these complications.

Pray that Bill's immune system will recover completely. The first three months after the transplant are critical.

Pray that a hospitality apartment will become available. We are on the waiting list for one of these apartments, which are available at no cost for us. Or pray for whatever God has planned for our living accommodation.

Thank you for walking with us through this journey!

Journey of Faith

Week of December 10, 2006

Thanks for your encouraging words and the support we have received this past week. We are reminded daily that we are not walking through this journey of faith alone; you are with us. God is so good, and He has blessed us with so many wonderful people who are praying.

We have more details about the week's schedule. Bill will be flying to Houston on Monday, December 11, and will undergo a full day of various tests the next day starting at 7:15 a.m. and finishing up at 8:45 that night. Many of these tests are a repeat of what he did in October. The doctors want to assess the outcome of the past two chemotherapy regiments. Wednesday he gets to rest and then will meet Thursday with two of his doctors for a final assessment and evaluation of readiness for the next step in the transplant process.

Initially Bill was to stay in Houston but was able to persuade his doctors to give him one more weekend in Tennessee. He will be flying home on Friday and will have another Sunday with our church family before the extended stay in Houston. Following the morning services, with our car loaded, we will make the trip to Texas.

Barbara will spend this week making final preparations for that extended stay. She has lots of packing to do but first must determine what to pack! She will finish up work at her job and plans to spend some time with the grandchildren during the evenings. Being away from those grandchildren for that long period will be hard, but we plan to take plenty of pictures.

Bill will be staying this week with our good friends, Joyce and Gary Aylor. Gary is the church administrator of First Baptist Church, Humble, Texas. This couple has opened their home to us, and we are deeply grateful.

We are claiming the following verse for the week: "The Lord is my rock and my fortress and my deliverer, My God, my rock, in whom I take refuge; My shield and the horn of my salvation, my stronghold. I call upon the Lord, who is worthy to be praised" (Ps. 18:2–3).

CHAPTER 11

Life Is a Daily Road Trip

My husband cannot believe I have somehow managed to close the car trunk. The backseat and even the floor of the passenger's seat are jammed to the limit with barely room for our feet. The car is finally packed after I made major adjustments, eliminating some of those possessions I was certain I might need but space would not allow. Bill and I check the house one last time before locking the door. It will be a long time before we return. I pick the Sunday paper off the grass tucking it under my arms. Bill climbs into the passenger seat, and I slide behind the wheel. The garage door comes down. As I drive out of the driveway, I see our home disappearing in the rearview mirror. Our road trip has begun, Sunday, December 17, 2006. We are headed to Texas!

Just thirty minutes into the trip and Bill is already asleep. He is physically exhausted from the Sunday morning services. His fatigue and my emotions have kept our conversation at bay. Only the movement of the car and the sound of CD music playing can be heard. I see on Bill's countenance a calm, blessed peace. Bill and I had knelt down beside our living room couch and prayed together just before we closed up the house. With our heads bowed and our hearts toward the heavenly throne, we had sought God's protection and guidance. Bill has found that rest beautifully described in Psalm 62:1–2: "My soul finds rest in God alone; my salvation comes from him. He alone is my rock and my salvation; he is my fortress, I will never be shaken."

Contrary to my husband's blessed assurances, I have this expanding knot in my stomach. The highway scenery drifts past unnoticed. My hands are on the wheel, my eyes on the road, but this time instead of a heavy foot on the gas pedal, my heart becomes the weighty one. My mind keeps controlling and wrestling with my emotions. This road trip to Houston certainly will be a journey I have never taken before. Houston is far from Nashville. I feel scared. Part of me wants to turn the car around and go back. Is this really the road we need to take? Lord you have put me on this path. Why am I doubting if this indeed is the way I should travel?

I have traveled down numerous roads in my lifetime and have encountered many potholes along the way. Life is like a road trip. Sometimes the road forks in directions that have left me confused, frightened, and unclear as to the exact turn I need to take. Some paths were like a highway, smooth and direct. Others were similar to avenues or streets filled with those potholes. Potholes can cause the roads to become bumpy and uncomfortable, like any unnerving trial. Today, the vagueness of what lies in front of me is keeping my compass cloudy, feeling like I am on the wrong road. At this point, I start looking for a possible detour sign, "Road under construction; go this way." Get us off this road! Maybe if I take another road, life will go back to where it was before.

The unknowns can be full of haunting "what ifs". But my Heavenly Father knows the right road I must take to get to the destination He wants for me. He often calls me to chart unknown territory as I follow Him and move out of my comfort zone. I must not fear; God has a view from above, an eternal perspective. He knows where He wants to take me, and what looks like a detour may actually be a new road to blessings.

I particularly question why this journey is taking me so many miles away from our home, family, and friends. Four, possibly five, months is a long time to be away from grandchildren, especially with grandchild number three on the way. I ponder the story about another senior couple's road trip. God told Abraham and Sarah to leave their comfort zone and travel miles away from their home, family, and friends to a land called Canaan. I wonder if Sarah had some of the same questions I'm having.

This couple went without knowing all the answers to their questions. I try to imagine how Abraham felt when God asked him to move his whole family without telling him where they were going. Their journey became a walk of faith as they entered uncharted territory. Oh Lord, don't let the fear of the unknown cripple my capacity to follow God's leading and help me to have the same kind of faith and to be obedient like Abraham and Sarah. They believed God. I need to just cling to the One who knows all things. I'm in good hands regardless of where God leads me. Nothing is too difficult for my Lord. God said He would direct Abraham. He said, "Leave . . . and go" (Gen. 12:1), and God said, "I will bless you" (Gen. 12:2). God's purpose in blessing one is to bless many.

How this road trip would bless me much less many is beyond my understanding, for right now my mind appeared to be stuck in a perpetual state of heaviness. On the outside I appear to have it all together, but deep inside I'm struggling. What if the transplant fails? A stem-cell transplant is a risky procedure. Over the past months my toothbrush has revealed my anxiety. Now my apprehensions are coming through like those neon signs on the highway, multicolors flashing in the dark. A load of uncertainties has imprisoned my judgment and thinking. Thoughts and questions keep rolling over and over in my mind like waves hitting the beach. Maybe I need to transfer my thoughts to the past instead of what lies ahead.

A smile crosses my face as I recall the jubilant time just week ago when Bill and I played with our two grandchildren while celebrating an early Christmas. The blissful joyful occasion will remain fresh in my memory making our separation somewhat bearable in the months to come. The children's excitement and amusement became a wonderful break from the many tasks that had consumed me over the past months. Their young, energetic, nonstop motion kept me busy the entire weekend. I loved every minute of it! I think their parents inserted some of those batteries that never run down because the night was late before they finally settled down.

I had decided not to lug all the huge boxes of Christmas decorations from the attic but to focus my time on making this festive event extra special for them. We made cookies and fudge, decorated Christmas ornaments, sang Christmas songs, read stories, and played games. Our family tradition of hiding gifts wrapped with children's games brought delightful laughter to their tiny faces. The grandchildren were given cues as they searched the house to locate the fun activities. Our house was filled with smells of baking cookies and the noises of giddy delights as the children played throughout the day. Having the children with us was good medicine for both Bill and me. It kept hidden my mounting worries and deep ache.

Bill read the Christmas story from the Bible later that evening with the children sitting on his lap. Then we all slipped to our knees beside the couch to pray. I had to swallow back my tears when Kayelynn prayed: "God, please make Papa get well. Let him come back soon." Kayelynn lifted her wide brown eyes in Bill's direction finishing her prayer. "Let Papa have hair. He looks better with hair."

When our prayers were done, I put the children on a blowup mattress next to our bed. Every time they spent the night with us, they wanted to be in our room instead of the guest bedroom located on the other side of the house. As I pulled up the covers to their little chins, Bill leaned forward and gave them each a kiss on the tops of their heads. "Good night," he said. Turning out the lights, all we could see was their bright, wide-open eyes and golden red hair. Bill and I heard the children giggling and whispering for several more minutes before they finally fell asleep.

I knew Bill had some personal thoughts he kept to himself as he lingered in his study late into evening. Would he get to celebrate the Savior's birth again with his grandchildren? Holidays have always been a special time for our family. We gather around our big dining room table to eat, tell stories from the past, talk about the future, and just enjoying one another's company. We spent Thanksgiving in a hospital, and now we would be spending another holiday away from family. Would Bill get to have another Christmas with us? A wave of sorrow came over me as I thought about missing another holiday with family and the lingering questions about the uncertainness of our future.

Driving down the highway, I had plenty of time to think. I mentally revisited my to-do list making sure I had not forgotten to do something. If I had, I didn't know what I could do about it now since we are well on our way to Houston. I had put together an extensive list over the past months. Placing it on the refrigerator door helped me focus on such things as shutting off the water, discontinuing the cable and telephone services, stopping the mail plus finding someone to water our plants and mow the yard. The list of things to do is long when you close up a house for several months.

My list aided me as I thought about what I would need for this trip. My thoughts kept turning back to Sarah when Abraham told her they would be leaving. What did she place in her backpack? Did she think about all she would be leaving behind? Did she get out her to-do list? My mind was going in so many directions as I prepared to begin this trip. I had so many things to do and so much to think about. I'm a task-list-orientated person so I would proudly checked off items as I accomplished them and then add more things to my list as I thought of them. My list kept growing!

Contrary to my husband's opinion, I approach packing in a somewhat systematic way. Of course I first made my list. Next I started gathering the items. I put them into containers marked winter clothes, spring clothes, books to read, writing materials, cooking essentials. I debated whether I needed the waffle iron or my favorite skillet! Finally everything was logistically organized and stacked in sections of our bedroom, kitchen, and hallways. Bill and I stepped over the piles for days. My husband did not say much about my piles of things, but I knew he was thinking, *How on earth does she think she can squeeze all of these possessions in the car, and does she really need all of this stuff?*

At last the day arrived, the day before we are to leave. I started lugging all those piles to the car. However, to my astonishment all I planned to take on this road trip would not fit into the trunk and backseat of our car. It's back to the drawing board to evaluate the situation. What could I leave behind? Should I leave the travel version of games such as Scrabble behind? I have been known to travel with more clothes than I really need.

Maybe I do have a few extra items on my list that are not necessary or indispensable for this trip. I'll confess, I am a pack rat, and I struggle with spendthrift impulses. My piles of things give evidence of this trait. I am always looking for a good deal even if I do not need the purchase. I enjoy rummaging through garage sells, finding treasures. My husband reminds me that our shared closet looks more like a ladies department store. He has been slowly squeezed out of space inch by inch as our closet—or should I say, my wardrobe—has maxed out. Why do I think I need so many things and can't do without them? After spending most of the day reducing my piles of stuff to a more manageable size, the trunk did close.

The hardest thing about preparing for a road trip is saying good-bye to friends and family. After fifteen years of working together, my coworkers are like family. My job and coworkers had become so much a part of my daily routine that I was not sure how I would adjust to a new schedule without them being around. Isn't it interesting how comfortable we get with our daily calendar and familiar friends that when life takes us down a different road we start to feel insecure and frightened?

My feelings were bouncing up and down like a rubber ball the Friday before we were to leave. My boss had planned a Christmas luncheon so we closed our offices early. I had cleared off my desk having completed all of the necessary arrangements for my absence. Turning off my computer and closing my office door brought the realization that it would be several months before I would return to my workplace. After eating at a local restaurant and enjoying fun conversations, the staff gave me a wonderful care package full of gifts. Overwhelmed with their kindness and expression of love, I found my eyes tearing up when normally I could control my feelings to some degree.

You already know I'm an emotional woman, but by the end of the day my tears were flowing like an open water faucet. Bill and I were going to have dinner with our children and grandchildren. This was the last time we would be together before leaving for Houston. Having to say good-bye became an emotional experience for all of us. Four months or longer sounded like such a long time. "Just keep praying," I said as I held my daughter's hand.

We stood in the restaurant parking lot after supper. For a moment we were silent just giving extra long hugs. Then our five-year-old granddaughter, Kayelynn, fastened her arms around Bill's legs and said, "Papa, I don't want you to go. I love you." It was hard for our grandchildren to understand why we were going away. They had repeatedly asked, "Papa, why do you have to go?" They knew their Papa was sick. He looked so different without his hair. But now it was Christmastime, and we were going away.

Bill gently lifted Kayelynn up, and she pressed her face against his. She stretched her arms around Bill's neck determined not to let go of him. That night Bill told each family member how much he loved them, and then we drove away wiping the tears from our cheeks.

The entire weekend had sapped me emotionally. Imbedded in my mind were the events of Sunday's morning services with our church family whom we loved dearly. Bill had preached his sermon knowing it would be a long time before he would see them again. Earlier Bill had written this note:

> **My deepest concern is the extended time that this series of treatments and ultimately the bone-marrow transplant will require us to be away. I can handle the health issue, but being out of the pulpit and away from you is my greatest challenge. Robert Murray McCheyne was forced to leave his pulpit in Scotland due to a serious heart malady and bemoaned the lost opportunity of preaching. Little did I know that some thirty-eight years after reading Andrew Bonar's account of McCheyne's life I too would be deprived of the privilege of preaching on Sundays. Be certain that as long as I am here and am able, I will be in the pulpit with a word from God on my heart. I will keep you informed about my schedule and travel to Houston as I know it myself.**

Before the worship service started, Bill had asked me to join him in his office to sign some legal documents. Our attorney had been finalizing several legal matters over the past month, and this appeared to be the only time we had left to complete the paperwork since we would be leaving right after the morning services. Sam, our attorney, also our dentist and a member of our church stood next to Bill. I sat in a nearby chair.

Sam had asked two other men to witness the signing of these legal documents. The room was silent as Sam read each of the three neatly typed documents bound on blue legal-size paper. As Sam read through each document, he asked, "Is this what you want?" Bill replied, "Yes."

I watched motionless as Bill signed his signature on each document. My eyes were fixed on him. I knew Bill had met with Sam to discuss his desires; however, I was hearing all of this for the first time. It sounded so final, especially now, having a last will and testament read. All of our married life we had discussed making a will but just never got around to it. What was happening in this office heightened my emotions and overwhelmed me as I realized once again that Bill might not survive this procedure. I could be returning back to Tennessee without my husband.

Sam read each document in his professional distinguishing voice.

The Last Will And Testament of William Henry Betts

I, William Henry Betts of Lawrenceburg, Lawrence County, Tennessee, do make, declare, and publish this my last will and testament. . . . I direct that all my lawful debts, including my funeral expenses and the cost of administration of my estate, be paid by my executrix as soon as practicable after my death. I bequeath to my wife, Barbara Joan Betts, if she shall survive me, all of my clothing, jewelry, personal effects, automobiles (together with any policies of insurance thereon), and all other tangible personal property owned by me at the time of my death. If my said wife shall not survive me, then I bequeath the above items of my personal property to my children, Jerram Christopher Betts, Regina Kaye Rathbone, and Geoffrey Wallace Betts, in equal shares share and share alike (with the issue of any deceased child to receive their parent's distributive share, per stripes).

The next document contained the "Durable General Power of Attorney" and the "Durable Power of Attorney for Health Care." Bill was giving me power and authority to handle any legal or business transactions and to have the power to make health care decisions for him. Each time Sam had asked Bill if this was his wish, Bill replied with the one word, "Yes."

My eyes were moist with tears as I sat frozen in my chair. The next section was the "Living Will." "

I, William Henry Betts, the declarant, willfully and voluntarily make known my desire that my dying shall not be artificially prolonged under the circumstances set forth below, and do hereby declare: If at any time I should have a terminal condition and my attending physician has determined there is no reasonable medical expectation of recovery and which, as a medical probability, will result in my death, regardless of the use or discontinuance of medical treatment implemented for the purpose of sustaining life, or the life process, I direct that medical care be withheld or withdraw, and that I be permitted to die naturally with only the administration of medications or the performance of any medical procedure deemed necessary to provide me with comfortable care or to alleviate pain.

Bill signed the last document.

The two men signed the documents as witnesses. I stood up and went toward Bill. No words were exchanged, for we both understood our emotions. Bill wrapped his arms around me. Our embrace gave me hope and strength in the quietness of the moment, for I knew what we had to do next would even be harder.

"Help me to stay strong and courageous, dear Lord. Give Bill the physical energy he needs to preach." I prayed silently. I wanted to make it through the service without falling apart, and Bill needed strength for his frail body. Every time someone hugged me, I started to tear up. At the conclusion of the service, our church family gathered around us for special prayer. The deacons laid hands on us while the church body prayed. I felt the power of God's love and the love of this special family.

Bill and I left the sanctuary renewed in spirit. We linked our hands together and walked across the parking lot in quiet solidarity. The strength of our relationship and the presence of God in our lives not only had sustained me throughout the morning but also will continue to give me power as Bill and I embark on a journey that would take us miles away from the familiarities and comfort of our families and friends.

CHAPTER 12

God's Provisions and Timing Are Perfect

It is day two of our Houston road trip. Bill and I decided to take the southern route to Texas driving through Alabama, Mississippi and Louisiana. The Bible says, "Cast all your anxiety on him because he cares for you" (1 Pet. 5:7). I'm doing a lot of casting as we travel down the unknown zones of human uncertainties. I have no idea what all Bill and I will face, nor do I know all God will do.

My concerns keep reverberating over and over in my mind. The feelings of uneasiness had turned to worries. Proverbs 12:25 says, "An anxious heart weights a man down." Contrary to a decrease in miles the closer we get to our destination, I'm experiencing a weight increase of a few extra pounds heavier since we started this trip. Feeling weighted down, an anxiety diet is needed.

God's Word tells me to turn my worries into prayer. "Do not be anxious about anything, but in everything, by prayer and petition, with thanksgiving, present your requests to God" (Phil. 4:6). According to Paul's advice in Philippians, I did not need to worry about anything, for my Heavenly Father is ready to listen to me. If I want to worry less, then I need to pray more! "Oh Lord, help me to cease any worrying and pray more. I know you have an apartment for Bill and me. Help me to trust you completely with this concern."

A Houston apartment had not become available in spite of being on the waiting list of several apartment facilities. The closer the time had come to our departure, the more worried I became. I had called faithfully each week to check on the status, but still nothing. Our dear friends Joyce and Gary Aylor, had insisted their home was open for us, but I knew Bill and I needed to be near the hospital. I prayed as I drove. God was about to show me once again that He cares for me, and His provisions would be more than I could imagine.

About mid-morning, Bill answered a call. After a brief hello he told the caller, "You need to talk to my wife." Bill knew this message was something I should hear firsthand, and he handed me the cell phone. "Hello, this is

Barbara," I said, holding the phone to my ear with my other hand on the steering wheel. "This is John from Hospitality Apartments. An apartment has just become available, and I want to see if you still need an apartment," the man stated calmly. As quickly as the words could roll out of my mouth, I said, "This is an answer to prayer. Yes, this is an answer to prayer. We have been praying for this. Our church family prayed specifically for Hospitality Apartments to become available. I can't believe this. Yes, we need an apartment." "Do you know when you will be coming to Houston?" the man asked. "We are on our way right now. We will be in Houston tonight. Oh, I can't believe this is happening. This is an answer to our prayers," I said, repeating myself with tremendous excitement.

I think I overwhelmed the man. He didn't know exactly what to say next except that the apartment would be ready that night. I quickly explained that we would be staying with friends that evening, but the next day, following Bill's tests, we would be ready to move into the apartment.

John told me a second time, "The apartment will be ready." I expressed my gratitude, "Thank you, thank you, the Lord has answered our prayers." I couldn't wait to share this news with our daughter. I called her immediately. "Regina, you are not going to believe what has just happened. We have an apartment!"

God's provision and timing were perfect in answering this prayer request in such a mighty way even before we arrived at our destination of Houston. Isn't it interesting how God can move His people out of our homeland, our comfort zones, and still provide completely for our needs in that transition process? When God tells me to leave one place, He already has provided another place. God told Abraham to leave, and he left without knowing exactly where he would end up. He was not even on a waiting list for an apartment, but he packed faith in his heart, obeyed, and left believing God for his provisions.

God calls his children to leave their securities and to step out in faith, believing God will take care of them. I'm not to worry but to trust and get excited anticipating what God will do. He makes all the provisions, for God is never aimless. He has a reason in His provisions as He shows me God is going to do what He is going to do, and He is going to do it right and good in His perfect time. God is all-knowing. He is all-seeing. He is all-powerful. He is in control of everything. He knows what we need and when we need it.

"Don't worry about your life, what you will eat or what you will drink; or about your body, what you will wear. Isn't life more than food and the body more than clothing?" (Matt. 6:25 HCSB). My Heavenly Father knew what I needed, and it was more than just an apartment. I needed to grow in trust and to depend on Him. I had become too comfortable and satisfied with my way of life. God knew I could benefit with this change of scenery.

Worrying didn't get me anywhere except more worry. God knows what I need better than I do. I have to remember that I always have enough when God is my supply. He desires for me to trust Him fully with my life. "But seek first the kingdom of God and His righteousness, and all these things will be provided for you" (Matt. 6:33–34 HCSB). "Do not worry about tomorrow; for tomorrow will care for itself" (Matt. 6:34 NASB). Carrying the worries, stresses, and daily struggles is not God's method for dealing with problems. He has a cure for my anxieties. Trust is the answer.

I needed not to submit to worrying but to submit to the Lord, who cares for me. God is in control of my circumstances so I do not have to be anxious about anything but only trust Him. Jeremiah 17:7-8 says, "Blessed is the man who trusts in the Lord, And whose trust is the Lord, For he will be like a tree planted by the water, That extends its roots by a stream and will not fear when the heat comes; But its leaves will be green, And it will not be anxious in a year of drought Nor cease to yield fruit."

I desired my trust to be like a tree planted by the water with my faith deeply grounded in Him who becomes the strength when those tests come around. I will not fear when the heat comes. Abraham and Sarah were tested along the way, but they went the distant even when they had serious setbacks in their faith. They struggled and waited for God's timing to be fulfilled. Sometimes they even made bad decisions by taking matters into their own hands, hatching a plan to aid the Almighty. I can identify with them. In spite of Abraham and Sarah's wavering faith, God kept His promises working on His timetable not theirs. I want to believe God and go the distant just like Abraham and Sarah.

Journey of Faith

December 22, 2006

Reflecting back on this first week of settling in Houston, Bill and I have so many things for which to be grateful to our Lord as He continues to show us His loving care. As we drove away from Lawrenceburg, Sunday afternoon, my heart was filled with many emotions. It was difficult to say good-bye to our church members, friends, and family. I knew it would be months before I would see them again. Bill and I prayed before leaving our home. Both of us know this is the journey God has prepared, and His peace that passes all understanding gives us the ability to move forward.

The Lord's timing is always right. His faithfulness in answering prayers came the next day. A call came in from Hospitality Apartments telling us they had an apartment available. The caller wanted to know when we would be in Houston. When I told them Bill and I would be arriving that night, they said the apartment is ready and we could move in anytime! You prayed for this apartment to become available, and the Lord answered by giving us a beautiful place to live for three months at no cost!

The apartment is completely furnished and is less than a mile from the hospital with shuttle services to and from the hospital. It cannot get any better than that! Hospitality Apartments is an independent, nonprofit, public foundation supported by foundations, individuals, corporations, and twenty-two local churches representing nine denominations. The apartments are for patients and their caregivers who need extended stay in the Houston area. It is totally managed by community and church volunteers.

Upon arriving at our apartment, we found a welcome bag filled with all kinds of goodies from the Joy Sunday School Department of Houston's First Baptist Church. We have met our neighbors, and everyone has made us feel welcome. I am learning about some of their health struggles as well. Our little apartment here reminds me of our first apartment as newlyweds during our seminary days. I have gone shopping and added a few little touches so it really feels like home for now.

I felt so comfortable and blessed in our two-room Houston apartment. The apartment was fully furnished with a couch, end tables, two lounge chairs, a kitchen table with four chairs, twin beds, and two dresser drawers. The kitchen cabinets were filled with the basic cooking utensils. A refrigerator, a stove with an oven, and a sink were positioned on one wall in the front room while the bedroom including a bathroom made up the second room. Our apartment was considered a luxury unit because we not only had a TV but also a VCR/CD player.

Paul's testimony, "I have learned to be content whatever the circumstances" (Phil. 4:11) has taken on deeper meaning in our simple abode. I discovered that I can survive without all my earthly bags of belongings I had accumulated back in Tennessee and even some of the things I had brought for this trip. I managed to cook and prepare meals without all those fancy electronic devises today's modern kitchens possess. I had two sets of sheets for the twin beds. When the sheets and towels got dirty, I did the laundry. With fewer things our tiny home became functional and efficient. I even found that I could get by with a wardrobe consisting of about five outfits. Now that's amazing!

During those months in Houston, I had plenty of time to do some reflection by taking inventory of what really is of value in life. I discovered that the most important things in life have nothing to do with the amount of earthly possessions people surround themselves with in their lifetime. All that material stuff is really not significant. I don't need all those unnecessary items I previously found essential to buy and own. The pursuit of things can consume my wishes and put me quickly in an "I must have" mode, distracting me from what is most satisfying in life, and that's relationships. I do not ever want to forget to live the simple life, clutter free, available to respond to the Great Provider who knows exactly what I need in this life and not what the world alleges I need. I need to set my mind on things above, not on things in this earth. Those who have their hearts fixed on heaven will hold loosely the things of earth.

From the start of this road trip, I saw many affirmations of God's faithfulness and power. God faithfully did what He promised. There is not a promise from God mentioned in Scripture that He did not bring to pass in His own time and in His own way. God is always faithful to fulfill His promises even when my faith is not as strong as He would like it to be. He provided for our provisions, and He demonstrated His love assured by divine ability.

"Being fully persuaded that God had power to do what he had promised" (Rom. 4:21).

"The LORD is faithful to all his promises" (Ps. 145:13).

"Let us hold fast to the hope we profess, for he who promised is faithful" (Heb. 10:23).

"I will never leave you nor forsake you" (Josh. 1:5).

"I will sustain you and I will rescue you" (Isa. 46:4).

"I will strengthen you and help you; I will uphold you with my righteous right hand" (Isa. 41:10).

"I am with you and will watch over you wherever you go" (Gen. 28:15).

"You are my hiding place; You preserve me from trouble; You surround me with songs of deliverance. I will instruct you and teach you in the way which you should go; I will counsel you with my eye upon you." (Ps. 32:7–8).

"Call to me and I will answer you and tell you great and unsearchable things you do not know" (Jer. 33:3).

"The Lord your God is in your midst, A victorious warrior. He will exult over you with joy, He will be quiet in His love, He will rejoice over your with shouts of joy." (Zeph. 3:17)

God took care of us by providing for all our needs including financial concerns. "And my God will meet all your needs according to his glorious riches in Christ Jesus" (Phil. 4:19). I knew our medical bills would be huge. I had questions about health insurance. What about all the expenses that come with having a major health problem? How will we pay all the bills? God showed me time and again that He will provide all we need at the time we need it. These Bible verses ministered to me. "But the plans of the LORD stand firm forever, the purposes of his heart through all generations" (Ps. 33:11). "A righteous man may have many troubles, but the LORD delivers him from them all" (Ps. 34:19).

Our church family demonstrated their support by continuing Bill's salary and benefits during the entire period of Bill's stem-cell transplant and recovery. We were able to pay bills, plus have the resources to live on while we were in Houston. Our daily bread needs were met by our Heavenly Father through our loving church members as they stood by us throughout our entire journey.

Bill knew this difficult trek would require a long stay in Houston, so back in November he had gone to the church deacons prepared to resign or take a leave of absence. His concern for the ongoing ministry of this church and his inability to fulfill his role as pastor weighed heavy on his heart. The deacons told Bill, "Resigning is not an option." They did not want Bill to leave. The chairman of the deacons later told someone there was never any consideration given for Bill to resign. "We knew the seriousness of the situation. The church was behind Bill and Barbara the whole time."

The people of God wrapped their arms around us and loved us. Bill and I were humbled by the generosity of kindness. This road trip was revealing God's amazing interventions. God was sustaining us in His Word with His glorious promises.

CHAPTER 13

Stem-Cell Donors Provide Hope

After giving birth to five boys, my mother-in-law decided she would just give up on having a little girl. She would settle for a houseful of rowdy boys and just wait for some daughters-in-laws to bring some order to the tribe. I can honestly say Mom treated me like a birth daughter. I had so much respect for this great lady and admired her steadfast commitment to raise her boys to be godly men.

Mom had a great influence on my life as well. She was my encourager during those early days of Bill's cancer before she passed away. I know she watched from the heavens with pride as Bill's brothers rallied around him eagerly ready to do whatever they could to save Bill's life. Bill needed a donor, and his brothers were ready to help. Which one would it be, one of three older brothers or the younger one? Bill's brothers were willing to give their stem cells, and that made this process even more exhilarating and emotional. To have this unique opportunity to give a gift of life is something that becomes an astonishingly beautiful expression of love.

To be a suitable donor, the genetic makeup of the donor's white blood cells must closely match Bill's, or serious complications could arise. Bill would be receiving an allogeneic transplant, which is when the patient receives a transplant from another person who is of the same tissue type, usually a related donor such as a biological parent, child, or sibling. Bill's siblings were tested for compatibility.

Brothers and sisters, who are born of the same parents, each have a 25 percent chance of being a suitable donor. That simply means a patient has a one out of four chance of being matched with a brother or sister. There is a much smaller chance of being matched with a parent, child, or distant relative. With four brothers, I calculated the odds of Bill having a match would be high. God had planned for my mother-in-law to have those five boisterous boys, and one would surely be a good match for Bill!

The brothers went through a HLA (Human Leukocyte Antigens) typing, a special blood test done to determine if one of them would be compatible with Bill's blood type. HLA is a genetic fingerprint on white blood cells and platelets, composed of proteins that play a critical role in activating the body's immune system to respond to foreign organisms. These proteins found in white blood cells make each person's tissue typing unique.

An HLA kit had been sent to the brothers, and once their blood had been drawn, the kit was mailed back to M. D. Anderson. We were told the results from HLA typing could take three to four weeks. The results came back sooner. Bruce, the second-born son, won the donor lottery. He became the perfect match having his tissue type 100 percent compatible with Bill's tissue. Bill's transplant donor had been found.

Stem cells can reproduce themselves as well as develop into mature tissues. When Bill and I were first married, we planted a garden by putting seeds into the soft ground. We watched as those seeds developed into delicious plants, reproducing more seeds. Stem cells are the "seeds" which produce the cells of the body. Every type of blood cell in the body begins its life as a stem cell. These stem cells then divide and form the different cells that make up the blood and immune system. Bruce's transplanted stem cells would provide Bill with a new blood and immune system and a chance for a new beginning.

In reviewing the past years of research, I learned there have been great strides in the donor process and transplantation of stem cells. During the 1950s through the 1970s researchers determined donor bone marrow cells infused intravenously could repopulate the bone marrow enabling the production of new blood cells.

Our doctor explained that M. D. Anderson performs hematopoietic stem-cell transplants. This means that hematopoietic stem cells are birth (natal) cells collected after birth from the umbilical cord or from the blood or bone marrow of a person. Hematopoietic stem cells are the critical cells for bone marrow or blood-stem-cell transplantation. There is one hematopoietic stem cell in every 100,000 bone marrow cells.

The first successful bone-marrow donor transplant took place in 1968. An infant with an immune-deficiency disease received a bone-marrow transplant donated by a sibling. Similar successes were reported in the years to follow. This type of procedure from a donor requires general anesthesia prior to the harvest. A doctor inserts a needle into the rear hipbone where a large quantity of bone marrow is located. Bone marrow could then be extracted with a needle and syringe. In order to extract sufficient bone marrow, several skin punctures and multiple bone punctures are usually required bringing some discomfort to the donor. Donors sometimes have legitimate medical concerns and emotional needs as they go through the process. Many times donors feel they have an enormous responsibility on their shoulders. I think that is especially true if the donor is a family member.

Later researched discovered that blood stem cells in the bone marrow could be moved to the bloodstream where they could be collected for transplant. The collection of stem cells this way produces more cells and does not require that the donor be subjected to general anesthesia to collect the cells from the bone marrow.

By the end of 1990s, many hospitals began transplanting patients with blood stem cells collected through the bloodstream. The donors would be given daily injections of a growth factor that would help stimulate the bone marrow to produce extra stem cells. These stem cells would then move and circulate into the bloodstream. The process used to collect stem cells from the bloodstream is called apheresis.

A central venous catheter (CVC) is used for the apheresis procedure. One end of the catheter will be connected to a machine that separates the stem cells from the donor's blood while the other end will be used to return the blood to the donor once the stem cells are collected in the machine.

Bill and I were thankful Bruce would not have to experience a bone marrow harvest, which is a surgical procedure that usually takes place in a hospital operating room, but instead his stem cells would be collected from the peripheral blood found in the bloodstream. When stem cells are collected from the bloodstream, they can be returned through the process known as a peripheral blood stem-cell transplant. Once the stem cells are put into a patient's body, they will begin to grow and reproduce.

In the beginning stages of stem-cell transplants physicians had to rely on autologous transplants, in which patients become their own donors. This type of transplant is performed when the patient's disease does not involve the bone marrow. Stem cells are removed and frozen, then the patient under goes chemotherapy and/or radiation to treat the cancer. The treatments are also designed to destroy any remaining stem cells. Once treatment is over, the patient's frozen stem cells are thawed and given to replace the stem cells that were destroyed as a result of the treatment. I have read that stem cells can be left frozen and stored for about five years. If they are stored longer, they are rarely used.

Bill's cancer was in the bone marrow, so an autologous transplant would not work for him. He would need an allogeneic transplant. The term *allogeneic* refers to a transplant from another person who would be a donor. The donor could be related or unrelated. Bill's donor would be a related donor, his brother. If Bill had an identical twin, he could have had a syngeneic transplant. This type has little risk of rejection since tissues coming from an identical twin are an excellent match.

An unrelated donor with the same tissue type would be called a matched, unrelated donor (MUD). M. D. Anderson was the first institution in Texas to perform a transplant using stem cells from an unrelated donor. Patients who need an unrelated donor might have to wait up to three to six months, and sometimes longer, to locate a match. I was glad Bill had a related donor, which would allow Bill's transplant to take place sooner.

M. D. Anderson uses a computer database with access to a central (national and international) bone marrow donor bank. The National Marrow Donor Program (NMDP) is a federally funded agency that coordinates the recruitment of unrelated stem-cell donors and facilitates transplants with unrelated donors. I read that over four million donors have voluntarily enrolled in the NMDP registry and more than one hundred transplant centers in the United States are authorized to perform transplants with NMDP donors.

Three days before Bill had his transplant, a twenty-eight-year-old woman received her stem cells from a donor from the European registry. A donor search initiated through the National Marrow Donor Program helped locate a suitable match. On the day of her transplant, her stem cells were flown into the Houston airport and delivered to the hospital by medical courier. Every year thousands of people donate stem cells to save the life of someone they love, and hundreds more donate stem cells for someone they don't even know.

Patients who do not have a donor may find a match through a cord blood bank. The term "cord blood" refers to the stem cells that are removed from the umbilical cord of a newborn baby. This type of transplant is called a cord blood transplant. After a baby is born, stem cells from umbilical cord blood are stored in cord blood banks. These cord blood banks have increased over the years. An advantage of using a cord blood bank is that the cord is available for transplant almost immediately. One drawback is that the number of stem cells available in one umbilical cord is low and may not be enough for a normal size adult.

Being a stem-cell donor is a wonderful opportunity to help save a life, and to give hope to patients diagnosed with diseases that were once thought incurable. For many patients a transplant is the only option for survival. I encourage everyone to consider being a stem cell donor. I thank you, Bruce, for being my husband's donor.

Journey of Faith

December 10, 2006
continued

Bill's brother and wife, Bruce and Karen, will arrive in Houston, Tuesday (December 12, 2007), to begin the seven–ten days of preparation for donating Bruce's blood and stem cells. Bill will be having an allogenic transplant, which means he will be receiving a transplant from a relative that matches his blood and tissue type. Many of you may not know that Bill is from a family of five boys. All of his brothers were willing to be donors and went through a HLA (Human Leukocyte Antigens) typing, a special blood test used to determine how compatible a patient and donor are for transplantation. If the donor and recipient are an HLA match, the risk of infection and "graft verses host" disease are less likely. The blood tissues and proteins are inherited from each parent, half from the mother and half from the father. The best donor for an allogenic transplant is an HLA matched brother or sister. Thank you, Bruce, for having the same blood and tissue type. You are giving Bill a new healthy blood system. Thank you for the wonderful Christmas gift!

The donation process involves a series of tests that Bruce will undergo followed by daily injections of a growth factor called Neupogen. This growth factor stimulates the bone marrow to produce extra stem cells that move and circulate into the bloodstream. He will be an outpatient making daily trips to the hospital for various assessments. On the seventh day his blood stem cells will be collected. This procedure involves separating and collecting the stem cells from the blood by using a cell separator machine and two intravenous needles, one in each arm. The donor is connected to a machine that will separate the stem cells from the blood and collect them into a bag. The remaining blood is returned to Bruce through the second IV. This procedure usually takes about four hours ,but may take longer. Bruce will stay longer if more stem cells need to be harvested.

God's ways continues to amaze us. Karen, Bruce's wife, is a kindergarten teacher and requested time off from work to be with her husband in Houston. The sub assigned to Karen's class asked to put Bruce and his brother on their church prayer list. During the conversation they learned that this lady was from Tennessee. She asked, "Where in Tennessee does Bill live?" Karen told her we live in Lawrenceburg. With that the lady said, "Well, that's where I used to live. What does Bill do?" Karen replied, "He is the pastor of First Baptist Church in Lawrenceburg." The lady continued by saying, "I used to belong to that church."

Journey of Faith

December 19, 2006

Tuesday was the day Bruce's stem cells were collected. Two more prayer requests have been answered. Bruce experienced a little discomfort and only a few side effects. He was able to produce over six million stem cells. Way to go, Bruce! Your brother will forever be indebted to you for the good job you did. We asked the medical team what would happen to any extra cells, and they said it would be saved for Bill in case he needed extra! After a final checkup on Wednesday, Bruce and Karen were given the OK to return to Tulsa. We were able to spend some special time together with them in the evenings and even found a great pizza place.

CHAPTER 14

Seeing Christmas from a Fresh Perspective

2006

When Jesus was born in Bethlehem, the people were busy traveling to the towns of their birth so they could be registered for taxes. It was a time of being with family and friends. Much food would have been consumed—not much different from today! No one seemed to be aware that it was a very special day on God's calendar, for it was the "fullness of time," and in the noise of the crowds and the celebration of family reunions, another celebration was going on in a quiet stable at the end of the Stable Lane. The only ones who came were Mary, Joseph and a host of angels. By the way, though the world paid no attention, the real Father was proudly watching the birth of His one and only Son!

This Christmas 2006, Bill and I traveled to Houston, to M. D. Anderson, a place far away from family and friends. There is no time and this is no place to be caught up in all of the commercialization of the holiday. And the things I usually do at Christmas will not be done this year—decorating the house, trimming the tree, and going to parties. How many times in the past have I come through the holidays in complete exhaustion, almost relieved that it's finally over and I can get back to normal? This Christmas is different! In the quietness of a hospital room, God gives me time to reflect on the true reason I celebrate Christmas. I celebrate the glorious gift of God, eternal life in Jesus Christ the Lord. God grants me a unique opportunity to see Christmas from a fresh perspective.

The first week in Houston went by rapidly with Bill preparing for his pre-transplant regimen. Bill and I are constantly going from one appointment to the next. Before being admitted to the hospital, Bill had to go through several tests and evaluation of his heart, lungs, and kidneys. These tests include blood tests, pulmonary function test, echocardiogram, electrocardiogram (ECG). Bill had to see an ophthalmologist because a side effect of a stem-cell transplant can cause damage to the eyes. It is important to have a baseline of

Bill's eye function. The doctors also have to assess a restaging of Bill's disease, which required Bill to have another bone marrow biopsy and computerized tomography (CT) scans.

I quickly learned the layout of the hospital floors and even some shortcuts as we met with doctors completing most of the initial procedures and the caregiver classes necessary for a transplant. What a blessing to have an apartment so close to the hospital. The hospital provides a shuttle service to and from our apartment on weekdays, and on weekends or late-night emergencies, we can call hospital security for transportation.

I find places in our apartment for the items I had packed in our car. I especially like the small walk-in closet, reminding me of the one back in Tennessee. The apartment manager has told me I can arrange apartment furniture to meet our needs, so I make a few changes. Our good friends, Joyce and Gary, bring over a card table and chair plus an additional lamp, which I set up in the bedroom corner for a computer desk. I found the Dollar Store and purchased a few items to brighten up our apartment, like a flower arrangement, placemats for the table, an area rug for the bedroom, and a curtain for the bedroom window. As Bill and I settled into Houston, our little apartment became our home. We feel comfortable. It is meeting our needs and giving us a feeling of security.

One blessing Bill and I encounter is the people we meet as our paths crisscross one another. As we wait for appointments, we have opportunities to talk with some of the patients and caregivers. Other times we might just make eye contact as we walk past them. A nod or a smile becomes a connection. I see patients walking down the halls in their robes while rolling their IV stands loaded with cancer-killing chemicals. Patients of all ages are bearing the marks of cancer in their bodies. A young girl with one leg hopples along on crutches and meets my eyes. My compassion and deep emotions reach out to her, wanting to encourage her as she struggles to balance herself. The people come from every corner of the world and from vastly different cultural and economic situations, but as they share their stories, they also share a strong fortitude. They are determined not to let cancer take their lives or their loved ones. Time after time we hear, "We're going to get through this. We will not be defeated by cancer!"

I have gotten acquainted with some of our apartment neighbors and the volunteers who give of their time managing the complex. These dear people have quickly become our new friends. Several of the residents have gone through a stem-cell transplant and are in different stages of recovery so we are learning much about the stem-cell process through their eyes. Others are in early periods of recovery and some are nearing the end of their hospital experiences. We meet others who are like us, still with many questions and somewhat frightened, feeling overwhelmed by all the information and possible side effects. As we share our common concerns and hopes for a cure, a sense of togetherness eases our fears and bonds us in a special friendship. We are not alone in this journey,

Journey of Faith

December 22, 2006

Our week started Tuesday morning when we arrived at the hospital at 7:30 a.m. and it finished up around 4:30 p.m. Every day has been filled with various tests and assessments. In preparation for radiation treatment, Bill underwent a simulation, which is a treatment planning or marking session. During this procedure the radiation oncologist locates the area to be treated, designs appropriate shielding for healthy tissue, and takes measurements for the treatment plan. He is actually fitted in a mold that will keep him very still during treatments. Bill is scheduled to have ten days of radiation treatment starting on Christmas Day.

Other procedures this week included surgical removal of the port that Baptist Hospital in Nashville inserted back in October and the insertion of a new Central Venous Catheter (CVC) with three ports. The CVC will be used for chemotherapy, blood products, antibiotics, and other intravenous medications. We were required to participate in two catheter care classes. I have learned how to flush Bill's port and actually did my demonstration test on Bill. Bill was somewhat nervous and would like me to participate in many more class before I do it solo! The infusion therapy nurse is giving me instructions on how to change the dressing, which has to be done weekly. The heparin cap is changed every two weeks when the catheter is not being used. Nurse Barbara is still learning how to safety do the many procedures!

Most of Thursday was spent at the Stem Cell Transplantation Center where we met with a team of doctors. They explained our options regarding Bill's participation in a clinical research study. We were told Bill's best treatment option would be this treatment plan due to current assessments that indicated his body and bone marrow still have cancer cells and the disease is still identified in many parts of his body. Bill will undergo a complex treatment prior to the transplant in order to attack the cancer and weaken his immune system, which may help the donor's stem cells to engraft in his body. This treatment regiment is designed to kill the lymphoma cells and to help reduce the risk of transplant rejection (graft versus host disease). Bill will have ten days of lymphoid radiation and will at the same time be given a drug called anti-thymocyte globulin (also called ATG). He will also have several treatments of rituximab (rituxam), a chemo that Bill has had several reactions to in the past. This study is new with plans for forty participants. Bill and I were told the risk involved, but we feel this is Bill's best option to be totally cured of the cancer. I recognize that everything is in God's hand and He controls the future. I'm confident God has the best for whatever that might be. My faith in my Lord Jesus has and will continue to lead me through this journey.

Bill will be admitted to the hospital on December 23 to begin treatments in preparation for the stem cell transplant, scheduled for January 5. Christmas Day will be spent in a hospital room. As Bill and I celebrate Christmas, our family and friends will be close to our hearts and thoughts even though we are miles apart.

I'm claiming the following verse for the week: "The LORD will keep you from all harm—he will watch over your life; the LORD will watch over your coming and going both now and forevermore" (Ps. 121:7–8).

This Week's Prayer Requests

1. Pray that God will give us many opportunities to share the gospel with the people that we will meet.

2. Pray that Bill can tolerate the rituxam and the other drugs with little side effects and that the radiation treatment will target only the cancer cells in his body without doing harm to his healthy organs and tissues.

3. Pray for Jim, a young man we met that will also be having a stem-cell transplant. He was told this week that he needed more treatments before the transplant. His father is the caregiver, and his mother is at home with MS (lots of medical issues).

4. Bill has had a persistent cough. Pray that he will be rid of the cough and free from any possible infections.

5. Pray for our daughter, Regina, who is pregnant with our third grandchild and experiencing daily fatigue.

We love you all. Thanks for your prayers.

Early Saturday morning, December 23, Bill and I emerge from our apartment, lock the door, and make our way to the hospital with a suitcase in tow carrying the necessary things needed for Bill's hospitalization. Caregivers are encouraged to stay with their patients, so I have packed a few of my belongings. The list of helpful items the hospital suggests to bring include personal items, soft comfortable clothes, a favorite blanket, books on tape, crossword puzzles, personal photos, stationery, and stamps. I feel confident I have packed the necessary items. Certain items are not permitted on the G11 floor such as fresh flowers, plants, and fruit baskets because they may contain bacteria and molds, which can increase the risk of infection.

Once we are assigned a room, I unpack our things in several drawers and a small closet. I become familiar with our new surroundings, trying to make the environment as organized as possible. I move the lounge chair closer to Bill's hospital bed. The nurse shows me how to pull down a bed from the wall unit, which proves to be comfortable. The hospital provides sheets, blankets, and towels, and I am allowed to use a guest bathroom just down the hall. The stem-cell transplant floor also has places designated for caregivers so they can have access to a refrigerator and a microwave.

Bill rests while nurses take vital signs and begin fluids through Bill's veins to ensure he will be adequately hydrated before his chemotherapy treatment. A medical team discusses and reviews Bill's treatment plan. Later Bill starts receiving his first chemo treatment.

In the evening while chemo flows through my husband's veins, Bill and I watch the Christmas video of Frank Capra's original *It's a Wonderful Life*, with one of my favorite stars, James Stewart. Each hospital room has a large TV with a VCR, and the hospital library provides videos we can check out. I have brought several of our favorites from home. As we settle into our dwelling place, I put a small Christmas tree in the window. The little lights give off a colorful glow. This quiet hospital room is where we will spend Christmas Eve and Christmas Day. We experience a peaceful rest that first night in the hospital.

I reach over and hold Bill's hand, and we listen to the CD player softly playing the beautiful song on Christmas morning. "Joy to the world the Lord is come"! Bill is resting beneath a warm blanket to knock his chill. After finishing his second round of chemo and his radiation treatment earlier, Bill has no energy, and he feels nauseated, having little desire for food. I keep a wet cloth over his forehead and an extra blanket over his feet. As Bill and I celebrate the birth of our Lord and Savior Jesus Christ, I read to Bill the passages found in Luke 2, and we talk about the gift God gave. God could not have given us a more perfect gift than His Son. Indeed this Gift keeps on giving and giving. Love never spoke so loud or ever expressed itself so fully as when the Christ child was born in Bethlehem. For good reason John wrote, "For God so loved the world, that he gave his only begotten Son" (John 3:16 KJV).

A hospital volunteer stops by our room later with a gift and an invitation to have Christmas dinner in the hospital cafeteria. I am hesitatant to leave Bill. He still feels dreadful with an increased amount of pain, but he encourages me to go. As I walk toward the dining area, the distinct aromas of turkey, dressing, and sweet potatoes evoke powerful memories and make my mouth water. I momentarily forget I'm in a hospital and recollect my past Christmas dinners where my family sits down around our large table filled with delicious foods. I enter the cafeteria to hear the sounds of Christmas carols being played as patients and family members share time together reminding me of how things used to be before we left our home in Nashville. I miss my family.

Volunteers serve the food. I don't think I have ever felt as loved as the volunteers give of their time this Christmas Day to share meals with cancer families who are miles away from their own families. What a gift! As I move through the serving line, one volunteer asks me if I am all right, for I have tears in my eyes and cannot hold back my emotions. I am not sure what I said to the man, but I am so overcome with feelings of praise and gratefulness.

The celebration of Christmas 2006 will forever be remembered.

Journey of Faith

Week of December 25–29

This Christmas will certainly go down in our memory as one of the most different we have ever experienced, but it will be a Christmas to be remembered, as Bill began his pre-transplant treatments. In our past, Christmastime has always been spent with family and friends sharing in those traditions that we have come to love. This year we celebrated in our quite hospital room with a small lighted Christmas tree placed in our window.

Thank you, Glenda and Chris, for the tree. It has reminded us of all our dear friends who have brought sparkle to our lives over these years. You all were very near and dear to our hearts, even though we were miles apart.

We have experienced moments that touched our hearts most profoundly. The fellowship and celebration that we shared with a caring nursing staff, the volunteers that served a Christmas meal to families and guests, the Christmas songs sung by our grandchild over telephone, and the quiet time we had to pause and thank our Creator for the countless blessings He has bestowed upon us are just a few of those memories. The Spirit of Christmas, which was born with a Babe in Bethlehem, dwells forever in our hearts. This Christmas we were mindful once again of

God's priceless gift: our personal Savior, Christ Jesus. God's love was with us this Christmas. "For I am persuaded, that neither death, nor life, nor angels, nor principalities, nor powers, nor things present, nor things to come, nor height, nor depth, nor any other creature, shall be able to separate us from the love of God, which is in Christ Jesus our Lord" (Rom. 8:38–39).

CHAPTER 15

Countdown: Preparation for Transplant

During the countdown period, usually the five to ten days before a transplant, a preparative regimen, which is also called the conditioning regimen, takes place. This is when doses of chemotherapy and/or radiation are administered. Bill will have a combination of chemotherapy drugs and a total of ten radiation treatments. The desired outcome for Bill is to destroy any existing disease in his body and to wipe out existing bone marrow cells in order to make room for new healthy donor cells where they will be able to grow and produce a new blood system. Bill's immune system will be suppressed so that the donor stem cells can engraft and begin producing healthy blood cells.

The body radiation treatments are taking place in the Radiation Therapy Center. This body irradiation involves the delivery of external beam radiation to certain parts of Bill's body. Bill's radiation treatments are designed to suppress the immune system and may help prevent rejection of the new stem cells. The suppression of the body's immune system and its ability to fight infections or disease is called immunosuppression. This immunosuppression can make Bill a high risk for infection, so Bill is receiving medications to lessen this risk and help manage the side effects of nausea. These past days Bill is experiencing some stomach and intestinal irritation, which does interfere with his ability to eat. He continues to lose weight, but his spirits are high.

Journey of Faith

Week of December 25–29

The first six-hour Rituximab treatment had few side effects for Bill. I thank God for His faithful people who have gone to the throne of grace on Bill's behalf. He is scheduled to have this drug once a week for four Saturdays. This therapy is designed to attach to lymphoma cells, which will cause them to die. On Christmas Day Bill had his first radiation treatment. The

Scriptures talk about bearing the marks of Jesus in our bodies. Well, Bill certainly has acquired a few more markings this week! His body has been marked using a special skin marker to outline the places throughout his body where he is receiving the radiation treatment. These markings and e-rays are made to ensure alignment to the areas needing treatment. By the end of this week, Bill will be halfway through with the irradiation treatment, and I pray continuously that those cancerous cells in his body will be destroyed.

I have been uplifted and encouraged in so many ways. For example, on the door going into our apartment closet are these words. "What Cancer Cannot Do! Cancer is so limited. It cannot cripple love. It cannot shatter hope. It cannot corrode faith. It cannot destroy peace. It cannot kill friendship. It cannot suppress memories. It cannot silence courage. It cannot invade the soul. It cannot steal eternal life. It cannot conquer the spirit. Cancer is so limited!"

In addition to the daily radiation, Bill is having about six hours of chemo (ATG), which has produced the normal side effects, nausea, vomiting, diarrhea, and abdominal discomfort. His blood counts have dropped so he was given a transfusion on Wednesday. Saturday's test results revealed that Bill has Respiratory Syncytial Virus (RSV). This is a virus that causes upper respiratory infection, most commonly occurs during infancy or early childhood, but can infect adults who have a low white blood count from cancer treatment. Bill may have had RSV for some time, which could explain his persistent cough. To treat this Bill has to remain in a tent that covers his bed while medication is breathed into his lungs. These three-hour treatments are done several times day and night for five days. No one can be in the room during these treatments, so I'm spending the nights at the apartment. Because it can be spread to other patients, Bill is in isolation: and anyone entering his room must put on a mask, gloves, and a long yellow gown. I look like Big Bird from Sesame Street!

I have managed to find the post office, grocery store, bank, and Target without the help of a Houston map. I'm feeling comfortable with the area and have walked several times to the hospital from the apartment. The weather is sunny and mild most days. I have told the apartment managers that I'm available to transport any residents without cars to the grocery store or to help with any errands. I'm finding this is a great way to meet and minister to our neighbors.

God is giving me peace each day, and He is filling it to the brim with possibilities. Certainly we face challenges, but I know His purposes are being fulfilled. God has blessed Bill and me beyond measure, and we owe

Him everything, including our praise. "Bless the L ORD, O my soul, and forget not all his benefits" (Ps. 103:2).

I'm grateful for your prayers. Prayer not only changes things; it also changes me as I turn every aspect of my life over to Christ Jesus. This journey of faith is a testimony to His love and to His grace.

Prayer Requests

1. Pray that the RSV infection will be eliminated and that Bill will not get pneumonia.
2. Pray for the final week of pre-transplant treatments that procedures will go well with no side effects due to the weakened immune system.
3. Pray for a successful stem-cell transplant scheduled for January 5.

I'm claiming the following verse: "Do not be anxious about anything, but in everything, by prayer and petition, with thanksgiving, present your requests to God" (Phil. 4:6).

Journey of Faith 2007

Week of January 1–4

There's something refreshing and optimistic about beginning a new year, full of promise and hope and visions of the future. Hanging a 2007 calendar near our apartment door will help me record daily appointments and mark off the days, bringing Bill and me closer to returning to Tennessee. The transplant book says Bill could possibly be in Houston one hundred days post transplant. I have counted out the one hundred days with April 15 marked with a large X. However, I believe Bill's recovery will progress more quickly allowing a March return. In the meantime I live from day to day in God's grace rejoicing in what He allows me to experience. I'm learning that God does not always take me out of problematic situations, but He gives the peace I seek as I proceed prayerfully through each day.

This week has been filled with many emotions. My mother fell and broke her hip on New Year's Eve. The surgery was risky due to her heart condition, but she survived in stable condition. My sister, Peggy, is with Mom, giving the comfort needed and communicating her progress daily.

I'm now more responsible for Bill's care since Bill was released from the hospital on New Year's Day. As an outpatient Bill goes back and forth to the hospital receiving radiation treatments and other pre transplant preparation procedures. Bill goes daily to the Ambulatory Treatment Center (ATC) section of the hospital where he will be monitored continuously up to transplant day and will be monitored for one hundred days post transplant. The ATC-bed units are designed to care for patients during the day, allowing patients to return to their Houston residence for the night.

Bill's blood counts have continued to drop this week. He wears a mask anytime we leave the apartment to prevent any possible exposure to germs. He has to be so careful not to get infections and is required to take special precautions. The RSV infection appears to be gone. That is an answer to prayer.

I have been given instructions to notify the medical team if Bill's medical condition changes in any way. If he has a fever over 100.5, I am to take him immediately to the Emergency Center. The pharmacist prepared fourteen medications that will help prevent infections, minimize side effects, and boost his immune system. I have the medications listed with the dosage and schedule tacked to the wall for convenient reference. Bill is now taking an immune-suppressant drug called Prograf to help prevent graft-versus-host disease (GVHD).

We continue to be impressed with M. D. Anderson Cancer Center's team approach in providing patient care. It truly is a multidisciplinary team made up of specialists in various areas who are involved in Bill's treatment plan. Bill has clinic doctors from the Bone Marrow/Stem Cell Transplant Center who oversees his daily treatment as well as a team of doctors from the clinical research study. He was seen by a number of doctors while in the hospital due to rotation schedules. Specialties have also made recommendations about his care.

It is the first time since Bill was diagnosed with Non-Hodgkin Lymphoma cancer some seven plus years ago that I now have a clearer understanding regarding Bill's cancer and how it has progressed. For example in the past Bill and I were given limited information regarding test results; however, now we are given written explanations along with the actual test results. We meet with professionals who make sure we have a clear understanding of Bill's health status and daily treatment plans. Advanced practice nurses, along with physician assistants and clinic nurses are working with the doctors in managing Bill's outpatient care. Bill and I feel involved in this process.

Test results from Bill's bone marrow have been diagnosed as chronic lymphocytic leukemia/small lymphocytic lymphoma (CLL/SLL). The blood cell-forming system in the marrow has become abnormal and malignant, which leads to an increase in the number of lymphoytes in the blood. The clinical research study that Bill is participating in is a treatment option with a special form of stem-cell transplantation that uses low doses of pretreatment radiation and chemotherapy to prepare Bill to receive the donor marrow. Bill will not have all his blood cells wiped out completely. The beneficial effects develop gradually over months and are thought to result from an immune attack by the donor's lymphocytes against the chronic leukemia cells. Eventually the donor marrow and immune cells become dominant. This approach is experimental, but doctors believe this is the best option for controlling Bill's disease.

You have joined me in praying for Bill's healing from this disease, and I believe that God will be honored in whatever the outcome. I know doctors don't heal us; only God can do that. God can and does use physicians and medical treatments in this world to effect healing. Bill and I have asked for guidance in finding the right doctors, which brought us here. The God of all hope is leading us, and we have hope for healing in this journey with cancer. It is indeed a journey of faith and hope. "May the God of hope fill you with all joy and peace as you trust in him, so that you may overflow with hope by the power of the Holy Spirit" (Rom. 15:13). "But now, Lord, what do I look for? My hope is in you" (Ps. 39:7).

Bill's transplant is scheduled for Friday, January 5. The procedure will take place at the hospital's Pheresis Hematology Center. Bill will have his last radiation treatment early; then the stem-cell transplant will follow. The afternoon could be spent in the ATC unit of the hospital receiving additional intravenous therapy. At the end of the day, we should be able to return to our apartment.

So much is still unknown about this progress. As Bill said to someone this week, it is not an event; it is a process. We sometimes don't even know what to pray for and just ask God to tell us how to pray. God's Word gives comfort. Romans 8:26 tells us that when we are in such a state, "the Spirit himself intercedes for us with groans that words cannot express." The Spirit prays for God's will for us when we don't have a clue what that is. And the Spirit "who searches our hearts" (v. 27) negotiates answers for us that far surpass anything we might have dreamed up on own. "In all these things we are more than conquerors through him who loved us" (v. 37).

CHAPTER 16

A Brother's Gift of Love

My human emotions were flip-flopping to opposite extremes the closer the time comes to the transplant. Not knowing what all we might encounter kept me edgy and jumpy. I didn't realize a body could manufacture so many emotions. I would be hopeful about knowing Bill might be cured but scared to death about what could happen if things went wrong. I knew we had done the right thing, but uneasiness remained. My apprehensions were like a roll of toilet paper. The closer it gets to the end, the faster it goes. My emotions accelerated as the date drew closer. Now, one day away from the transplant, I was having serious doubts about the original decision to go forward with the procedures. I lay the thirteen-page document with its detailed description of the treatment plan and the consent forms on top of the bedroom dresser drawer. These past days I have read it several times.

I lay back on my bed, staring at the document. Several pages contained information about the risks, side effects, and discomforts to the participants. It states the potential benefits on the last page. "The treatment may help to control the disease. Future patients may benefit from what is learned. There may be no benefits for you in this study." Wow, not a lot of encouragement from that last sentence as I pull the blanket over my shoulder against my feeling of chill in the room.

All of my doubts and questions stab at my innermost being. I can't contain all this nervousness. Gritting my teeth as I curl up on my side, I keep replaying in my mind the conversations Bill and I had with the research study staff when they explained why this research protocol had been selected. Bill had certainly met the criteria for this particular study because he has non-Hodgkin's lymphoma, chronic lymphocytic leukemia, and he needed a stem-cell transplant.

Bill and I were told the stem-cell transplant could replace his defective blood and immune system. I learned that Bill would be the fifth patient to go through this particular clinical trial. I recalled shifting in my chair as I asked the doctors, "How did the previous four patients do with the treatment plan?" One replied, "Two of the patients have done very well, but the other two have not done as well." I wasn't sure what all that meant, but 50 percent didn't sound all that encouraging.

"Lord, let Bill's treatment be successful." I had silently prayed as Bill signed the consent form. The doctors told us that all patients who participate in this clinical study would be treated in a uniform manner. That simply means they will receive the same treatment plan and then the results, after being collected and studied, would be published in a scientific journal. The goal of this particular clinical research study is to see if combining this specific radiation therapy, chemotherapy, and a blood stem-cell transplant can help control certain types of leukemia or lymphoma as well as studying the safety of the treatment.

Stem-cell transplantations can be a risky procedure due to the many possible complications and can even turn on patients attacking their skin and organs. Because of these possible deadly complications, stem cell transplants are usually reserved for patients with life-threatening diseases. In those early years some patients were cured, but many died. It was estimated that one out of three patients did not live past the first three to six months post transplant.

The chemotherapy regimens associated with the procedure were often highly toxic. Leukemia patients like Bill usually need the high doses of chemotherapy in order to eliminate malignant cells. Bill's protocol would be using lower doses; however, it is still considered a high risk procedure. I know it is Bill's best option for remission, especially since he is not responding to other regimens.

I do feel encouraged due to the many strides that have been made in the stem-cell medical field as a result of clinical research studies and major breakthroughs in addressing early problems. Many physicians have also discovered how to administer effectively the chemotherapy and radiotherapy regimes that precede the infusion of stem cells, resulting in less toxicity and fewer treatment related deaths. With a more precise and accurate dosing of intravenous treatments, doctors are able to monitor closely drug levels in the body. All of these medical advances give greater outlooks for patients who need an effective therapy for long-term disease control.

Bill's stem-cell transplant will come from his brother's stem cells. This type of stem cell is sometimes referred to as adult stem-cell transplant. Bruce's healthy blood stem cells will infuse into Bill's bloodstream where they will find their way into the cavities of his bones. The stem cells would then take up residence in Bill's bone marrow where they will begin producing normal blood cells, circulating in Bill, giving him new life and hopefully destroying any remaining cancer cells. When the stem cells are collected from the bloodstream, it is called a peripheral blood stem-cell transplants.

Unlike embryonic stem cells, these stem cells in research and therapy are not controversial because the production of stem cells does not require the destruction of an embryo. At the time of Bill's transplant, M. D. Anderson did not perform embryonic stem-cell transplants. Embryonic stem cells are those that are removed from the early embryo and are programmed to rapidly form a variety of tissues in the body.

Having a strong belief that embryos are human beings and have a right to life, I have a problem with taking a life in order to prolong a life. I believe that human life is sacred and life begins when a sperm cell fertilizes an egg cell to form a single cell. Conception marks the beginning of human life. "For You formed my inward parts; You covered me in my mother's womb. I will praise You, for I am fearfully and wonderfully made; Marvelous are Your works, And that my soul knows very well" (Ps. 139:13–14 NKJV). God fashions a tiny body together in the darkness of a mother's womb. All human life, the born and those still in the womb are unique productions of our Creator's genius.

God is pro-life, for all life is created by God and bears His autograph. The Scriptures teach that God not only created life, but gives life, sustains life, and takes it away. I'm aware of the many ethical debates about stem-cell research involving the creation, use, and destruction of human embryonic stem cells. I firmly stand on the position that human life must be preserved. If stem cells from embryos are used, I strongly believe it must be done without killing the embryos. An embryo is actually a human, and it should be valued as highly as all human life. I believe that human life is created by God in His image; therefore, I will defend, protect, and value all of life.

I'm so thankful new insights are being discovered each year regarding stem-cell research. The recent discoveries from scientists in November 2007 have found different genetic recipes to give ordinary skin cells the power to turn into virtually any kind of human tissue, just as embryonic stem cells do. If the recipes live up to their promise, they could someday end the ethical debate over embryonic stem cell research and usher in an era when a person's own cells can be manipulated to mend a broken spinal cord, heal a damaged heart, or regenerate other failing tissues.

I think we are probably still years away from seeing how this will impact disease treatment. However, I believe in time stem cells will be extracted without destroying embryos and there will be the potential to grow batches of cells from adult cells that will be able to repair or replace damaged tissue, thereby reversing disease and injury. In fact, it is estimated that stem-cell research will have the potential to help millions of people who suffer from diseases and injuries. Already, stem-cell transplants have become a viable option in confronting a wider array of diseases such as sickle-cell disease, myelodysplastic syndrome, neuroblastoma, lymphoma, Ewing's Sarcoma, Desmoplastic small round cell tumor, Hodgkin's disease, and multiple myeloma.

———

In the world of transplant, today is called "Day 0." It is January 5, 2007. Bill will receive his stem cells. The following days after transplant will be noted as day (plus) 1, day 2, day 3, and up to one hundred days post transplant. Bill completes his pretreatment transplant phase in the morning and by the afternoon his stem cell infusion begins. Day O marks the end of the countdown and the day of transplant, but I call this day, "A Brother's Gift of Love." New stem cells travel through my husband's bloodstream giving new life to a blood system that could no longer sustain life.

I feel my stomach tightening as I sit quietly in a chair next to Bill. The doctor explains each step of the process. As I listen, I also pray silently: "Lord, you love Bill. He is in your hands. I give him to You to do whatever You want with his life." I know God wants my faith even when I cannot see what all lies ahead. Some things are known only to God. When it comes to understanding the ways of God, those things can defy human understanding. What God does cannot be gauged in my college science lab or scrutinized under a microscope, for God does not always do things in an easily explainable fashion. Today I'm only seeing a part of the picture. My childlike trust has limited vision, but I know who knows what lies ahead so I can rest in His love regardless of what forecast is made or what complications arise.

Journey of Faith 2007

January 5, Transplant Day

I cannot go to bed tonight without letting you know our deep gratitude for all your prayer support. Our dear church family had a continuous twenty-four-hour prayer chain starting at midnight. We have been touched by all the love and have felt a great peace about this day. You held us up in prayer, and God heard you. Your prayers reached heaven, God's holy dwelling place.

We praise the Lord for His surpassing greatness and what He did today. We count it all joy to have walked through this day knowing this is a new beginning for Bill. I will give you bits and pieces about today, but I'm sure only God knows the full impact that will be revealed in God's timing and for His glory.

The day started early and is probably one of the reasons Bill has been sleeping most of this evening. He has felt fatigue with continuous nausea and been unable to eat for several days, but his spirits are high as he always thinks of others above himself. He is my inspiration and earthly rock. If you are the shuttle bus driver, a nurse, or just someone we happen to meet, Bill always has a positive word and a smile on his face. That's just one of the reasons I love him so much.

Our first stop today was the Radiation Treatment Center, where Bill had his last radiation treatment. The nursing staff has a tradition they do when a patient finishes the last treatment. The patients get to ring a bell that can be heard in the waiting room. When Bill entered the waiting area, everyone clapped. Memories of this trip will forever be imprinted on my heart, but one I shall always remember was the man without a face. Cancer had destroyed most of his face. He had no nose, just a few marks that resemble a face. Yet this man clapped his hands in honor of Bill's accomplishment. I have seen bodies that are fading and faltering, but spirits that are renewed. Cancer is limited; it cannot conquer the Spirit.

I have a greater understanding and appreciation for Leviticus 17:11: "For the life of the body is in its blood. I have given you the blood on the altar to purify you, making you right with the Lord. It is the blood, given in exchange for a life that makes purification possible" (NLT). Through Jesus Christ giving Himself as a sacrifice, shedding His blood for sinners, we can have forgiveness and eternal life. His blood is life, eternal life. We are experiencing that life abundantly because of the blood of Jesus Christ.

Today, as I watch new blood stem cells transfused into Bill's body, that verse becomes more meaningful. I thank God for the blood Bill's brother, Bruce, gave to Bill. Bruce gave his blood, stem cells, in love, a sacrifice of love. He gave it so that Bill could have new life in his earthy body. Cancer was destroying Bill's blood system, but now new blood is flowing through his body, giving Bill life for this world. "For the life of the body is in its blood."

The transplant process started about 1:00 p.m. with the first bag of stem cells given to Bill around 2:00 p.m. Bill was given four bags, each taking about thirty minutes. The transplant was given like a blood transfusion. A total of 6.7 million cells! God knows each and every one of those cells; isn't that amazing! The stem-cell bags are kept frozen in a metal container. Each container had Bill's name, his hospital ID number, Bruce's name, and the date the stems were collected. The staff checked identification each time the stem cells were handled to ensure safety.

The cell bags were put into a container called a "water bath" where they were defrosted at body temperature. This was done when one bag was empty and Bill was ready for the next. By 4:00 p.m., all of the stem cells had been given to Bill. He was comfortable and slept most of that time due to the premeds. Bill was monitored for an hour after the transfusions; and since there were no signs of rejection, we were allowed to return to our apartment. It was a simple procedure but one that I shall always remember. There is truly life in the blood. I witnessed that life being put into my husband's body. Thank you, Lord, it has been a good day!

From the beginning of this cancer journey, Bill has claimed and quoted to me that beautiful verse in Jeremiah 29:11: "'For I know the plans I have for you,' declares the LORD, 'plans to prosper you and not to harm you, plans to give you hope and a future.'" In that hope our spirits are renewed, and we trust Him, for His plans are always the best. Tomorrow is Day 1. The first day post-transplant! We start counting those days off and look forward to seeing God's plan revealed daily.

CHAPTER 17

The Wait Begins
Reflections from the Journey, Days 1–15

It is one week after transplantation, day 7. Bill's energy level plummets as he deals with all the physical discomforts associated with a transplant experience. He is experiencing the full effects of the chemotherapy and radiation. Feeling sick, unable to tolerate certain foods, Bill's appetite continues to decrease. He is losing weight fast. Besides the constant fatigue, he looks pale, weak, and lifeless. I try to get him to eat, especially high calorie and protein intake, by bringing him milkshakes loaded with calories. With the aid of anti-nausea drugs, the nausea and vomiting are to some extent controlled. One day Bill feels much better only to awake the next day feeling tired, sicker, and weaker. The physical battle taking place between Bill's diseased blood cells and the new healthy ones is like a roller-coaster ride.

Bill and I were told the two- to three-week period after his transplant would be a critical time. Serious and frequent complications due to Bill's weakened condition after so many years of failing health could delay recovery. The treatments before the transplant have destroyed most of Bill's blood stem cells, temporarily crippling his immune system. Until Bruce's new stem cells migrate to the cavities of Bill's bones, engraft, and begin producing new healthy blood cells, Bill could be very sick and would have very low blood counts making him highly susceptible to infection and possible excessive bleeding. These setbacks could be serious.

During this critical period Bill receives multiple transfusions and antibiotics to ensure special precautions are taken to prevent infections. The doctors give these medications to help lower the likelihood of developing graft-versus-host disease. Bill's body is not able to maintain safe levels of circulating red blood cells and platelets, so the transfusions support his body until his blood counts recover. The need for a blood transfusion is determined by Bill's hemoglobin value. I learned that the hemoglobin is the substance that carries oxygen in the cell and that normal adult hemoglobin level is between 12 and

14. When Bill's level drops below 8, he is given a blood transfusion. Normal platelet counts range from 150,000 to 450,000. When Bill's platelet count drops below 10,000 or if he is experiencing signs or symptoms of bleeding, he is given a platelet transfusion.

Every day blood samples are taken to determine whether the stem cells have engrafted and also to monitor blood counts and any effects the pre-transplant treatments might have had on Bill's organs. These weeks are physically, emotionally, and psychologically taxing as I wait for the transplanted stem cells to engraft and for blood counts to return to safe levels.

Journey of Faith 2007

Week of January 7

It has been one week since new stem cells were infused into Bill. The stem cells collected from Bruce's blood are now going through Bill's blood, making their way to the large cavities of his bones where they are encountering Bill's diseased bone marrow. Now the fight begins between the old and new blood cells. The battle will begin first in the bone marrow as the new stem cells find a nesting place to reproduce and become dominant, attacking Bill's remaining diseased cells with healthy cells.

The bone marrow is the spongy tissue found inside large bones, such as the hip and breastbone. It is in the bone marrow where stem cells are produced. Stem cells are immature forms of the cells that make up our blood. Without bone marrow and the disease-fighting blood cells it produces, the immune system would be severely impaired and would have little defense against even the most common infection. This is why any change or disease in bone marrow function can be life threatening and is one reason Bill needed a stem-cell transplant. Bill's new stem cells will begin to grow (engraft) and produce new cells. Bill has experienced discomfort this week in his large bones, which is evidence that the battle has begun.

This battle will continue for many days and months. Doctors have warned us to expect good days when everything appears to be on track as well as possible setbacks when things begin to go wrong in his body. This is all part of the battle. For two days this week Bill felt great, had good appetite, and everything appeared to be progressing according to schedule. He only needed one blood transfusion on Wednesday. With his blood counts dropping, Bill is getting weaker.

Late Wednesday evening Bill experienced a low-grade fever, and by Thursday it escalated to the point that he had to be moved from outpatient to inpatient status. He was readmitted to the hospital transplant floor (Gll) and put in a protective environment room. Because his resistance is low and showed signs of some kind of infection, the doctors wanted to give him stronger antibiotics to fight in this battle. On Friday, Bill received two pints of blood and one platelet transfusion. The new stem cells have not made enough white cells at this point, so Bill is getting more antibiotics. The doctors have assured me that this is not uncommon in this early stage of stem cell transplant, and I know God is still in control of this process. I'm somewhat relieved that Bill is in the hospital 24-7 because he will be receiving the best care during these next few days.

Remember, Bill was given a total of 6.7 million stem cells to fight in this battle! So as these new stem cells reproduce themselves and develop into mature tissues, they will win the battle. They will become the "seeds" which produce new cells for Bill's body. When released from the bone marrow, stem cells then divide and form the different cells that make up our blood and immune system. These include white cells that fight infection, red cells that carry oxygen, and platelets that prevent bleeding. A simple way to explain the medical objective is that when this battle is over Bill will have a new blood system to control the cancer cells. One nurse explained it this way: Bill will have had a genetic remake at the blood level. Bill's blood level (DNA) will be 100 percent like Bruce, his donor and brother. He will have healthy blood cells! To God be the glory for His infinite ways of working in us.

As all of you know, I have limited medical knowledge, so all of the above is my feeble attempt to explain what is happening. I think about a spiritual application Bill and I discussed this week. The fight that is taking place in Bill's body is similar to another battle Christians face. Galatians 5:16–18 talks about two forces that are constantly fighting each other, the Holy Spirit and our old way of life. Colossians 3:5 tells us to put to death the sinful, earthly things lurking within us. Ephesians 4:22–24 tells us to throw off our old flesh and our former way of life, which is corrupted by lust and deception. Instead, let the Spirit renew/ transform our thoughts and attitudes. Put on our new nature, created to be like God, truly righteous and holy.

"Fight the good fight of faith, lay hold on eternal life, to which you were also called" (1 Tim. 6:12 NKJV).

"I have fought the good fight, I have finished the race, I have kept the faith" (2 Tim. 4:7 NKJV).

The Lord stands with us in every battle we face. He enables us to get through every difficult situation, as we fix our eyes on Him, trusting Him to win our battles.

Tomorrow (Saturday, January 13), Bill will have his last scheduled Rituximab treatment. Pray that this chemo drug will go directly to any remaining cancer cells that have lingered in Bill's body, destroying them completely. We hold on to God's promises; He is our strength.

> Praise the LORD, O my soul,
> and forget not all his benefits—
> who forgives all your sins
> and heals all our diseases,
> who redeems your life from the pit
> and crowns you with love and compassion,
> who satisfies your desires with good things (Ps. 103:2–5).

I find myself watching and waiting once again. It appears to be a part of my life. I wait for the hospital shuttles, the test results, the doctors, the blood counts to climb, the nausea to go away, the fatigue to lessen, the day Bill can leave the hospital, and ultimately the day Bill and I can return to Tennessee. Without a doubt the biggest challenge for me is waiting for the stem cells to engraft. How long will it take for the stem cells to be accepted by Bill's body and start producing those new blood cells? This waiting contributes to my posture of helplessness, keeps me feeling powerless, so vulnerable not knowing what unforeseen complications might be around the corner.

Journey of Faith 2007

Week of January 14–19

The sense of time radically changes during these days of waiting for Bill's blood counts to move from the critical stage to normal. Sometimes I feel time seems to stand still as I wait for changes. Day after day for five days white counts had remained at an all time low of 0.2. During the wait and those anxious moments, it seemed as if all the clocks in the world have forgotten how to move their hands. How long is it going to take before Bill's counts begin to go up? Each time we see the blood report, I wait another day! I ask, "How long will it take?" The Bible calls these troubles "momentary," but to me they often seem to last forever. The Psalms are a great place to turn when I am waiting, needing encouragement, and especially Psalms 13. Four times the writer asks, "How long?" I can really identify with this writer, for David asked this question during his struggle from relief and concluded with verses 5–6. "But I trust in your unfailing love. I will rejoice because you have rescued me. I will sing to the LORD because he is good to me" (NLT). Help me to continue to trust God even when He doesn't answer immediately. God has been good as He turns my waiting and anxious moments into hope and trust. He fills me with His assurances that the waiting is apart of His plans and the need for faith in God's timing.

On Wednesday I saw some indication that Bill's white counts were beginning to recover. They were 0.3; Thursday, 0.4; and today, Friday, 0.4. Small increases but still encouraging! The first sign of a successful transplant is an increase in the number of white blood cells (the cells that protect your body from infection). Today, is day 14, (14 days past transplant), and as Bill improves, his blood cells and platelets will continue to grow in number. I'm not sure how long I will have to wait until Bill's counts return to normal, but God is providing abundantly in this wait time. This journey will lead me always to Him.

The dangerously low blood counts have necessitated blood transfusions. Bill has received five blood transfusions and one platelet transfusion since being admitted to the hospital. M. D. Anderson Cancer Center uses more blood products than any other facility in the Texas Medical Center. Bill also receives daily intravenous fluids helping with the adjusted blood levels and antibiotics assisting with his immune system. We are thankful that Bill had no side effects with the last rituximab treatment.

During this stage Bill is at great risk of infection, so he was placed in protective isolation. In this controlled environment he is protected from others' germs of others, and other patients are protected from any infection he might have. There is still concern that the RSV may still linger in his body. The protective environment room has a higher efficiency air-filtration system that provides optimal protection against organisms by using positive pressure and frequent air exchanges. To get to his room you go through an outer room, where any person that enters his room must put on gloves, gown, and a mask. These items are discarded in a box before leaving.

This protective environment is similar to the protection God gives. "Guard me as you would guard your own eyes. Hide me in the shadow of your wings" (Ps. 17:8 NLT). The "shadow of your wings" is a figure of speech symbolizing God's protection. He guards us just as a mother bird protects her young by covering them with her wings. God spreads His protection over us. God's protection is limitless, a safety fortress, a place where the enemy can't follow, a shield of love that comes between us and harm. Bill is protected in this controlled hospital environment and completely protected in the shadow of God's wings.

After days of hospital life, we've settled into a routine that looks somewhat the same each day. Bill is weighed every morning, helping doctors see how well he is responding to IV fluids and making sure he is getting calories. Throughout the day his intakes and outtakes are measured and recorded. He is expected to do mouth care every two hours by rinsing with special solutions. Good mouth care can decrease the chance of mouth sores and promote healing. Bill does breathing exercises, using an incentive pyrometer, at least four times a day. This helps to expand the lungs and prevent pneumonia.

The nurses check Bill's vital signs at least every four hours, and throughout the day he receives oral medications. The nurses are assigned only three patients each, enabling excellent care. Between 5:30 a.m. and 6:00 a.m. blood is drawn ,and results are available by mid-morning. The doctors arrive around 9:00 a.m.

Meals can be ordered through room service anytime Bill wants to eat. I can also order from the guest menu. Bill cannot have certain foods such as fresh fruits or vegetables. Meat and fish have to be fully cooked; however, he cannot eat any shellfish. Even though he can choose from a variety of foods, Bill has little appetite. He has been eating such small portions due to some nausea. I walk to the hospital every day around noon, bringing the mail. We open and read each card and feel blessed to have such a host of people praying and encouraging us in this journey. Bill has time for naps in the afternoon. The best thing about this hospital confinement is that both of us are having some quality time in the Word, enjoying quiet time, and studying. Bill is preparing a Bible study on 1 Peter.

Patients are encouraged to exercise by walking around the G11 floor. This hospital floor is for BMT patients only, so they limit visitors, and no children are allowed. There are fifty-two BMT rooms, divided into four nursing pods with each pod having its own nursing station. If we walked around the pods five times, that's a mile. We have accomplished several miles this week. Bill's walking attire is lovely—a long yellow gown, gloves, mask, and IV tree with four pumps.

Our entertainment this week was John Wayne's old western movies. All we were missing was the popcorn! I usually stay until 9:30 p.m. and then return to the apartment using the hospital transportation services. The day ends when I call Bill to let him know I made it back to the apartment safe and sound. We confirm our love for each other as we say good-night. Tomorrow is a new day, and we will rejoice and be glad.

That's a glimpse of our hospital routine.

We have some grandparents' news. Our daughter and son-in law will be giving us another grandson. Jacob Daniel Rathbone will arrive in June.

We had two special visitors today, Joyce and Gary Aylor. They looked real cute wearing yellow gowns, gloves, and masks!

Bill and I love you and thank you for your prayers.

CHAPTER 18

The Sun Is Shining Somewhere
Reflections from the Journey, Days 16–24

Cold air leaks through my jacket while the rain hits my umbrella. I tighten my grip, but the wind blows, flapping the ends of the umbrella. I shiver as the wetness hits my warm skin. The wind-blown rain hits my unprotected legs. My eyes are focused on the familiar pavement as I make my daily walk to the hospital. Dark, ominous storms have invaded the city of Houston, keeping the sunshine captive and hidden from sight.

The stormy weather—cold, wet, and rainy days—takes me deeper into an unsettled feeling of gloom. The constant downpour of rain and the darkened sky have engulfed my emotions, clouding out any peep of light and optimism. Just when I see glimpses of sun starting to shine, another cloud appears, ushering in more disappointments. Bill's blood counts have dropped dangerously low, and the forecast does not look good. His body is weaker and sometimes even lifeless. "Oh God, take Bill and me out of this storm. Make the sun shine." I don't like these adversities. I cry out in despair, and my tears mingle with the raindrops slowly falling to the wet ground beneath my feet.

Each day I dry off, regaining confidence, but the winds keep blowing, and more rain keeps coming, dashing my hopes. I cling to my human securities until I finally release my control. I confess, "I cannot do this anymore!" If one more thing happens, I am going to fall apart. Bill's immune system is dreadfully weak, and his blood counts aren't coming up. I'm afraid. I do not have the strength to handle this. I do not need to pretend that I have it all together. I have no more physical or emotional stamina left. I surrender.

Something wonderful happens. God reaches from the heavens and calms the storm, settling my heart. The Holy Spirit whispers to my innermost being. "I am in charge. Just trust Me. I know you can't handle all of this. Give it to Me." In humbleness and contrite spirit, I admit my lack of faith. I once again release everything into the Lord's hands. God extends His tender mercies and grace, giving me strength to go on. I feel the gradual release of my apprehension. I'm going to survive these stormily days.

"God, save me, because the water has risen to my neck. I'm sinking down into the mud, and there is nothing to stand on. . . . I am tried from calling for help; my throat is sore. . . . God, because of your great love, answer me. You are truly able to save" (Ps. 69:1–3, 13 NCV). Every time those storms came and the doubts would rise I felt like I was sinking fast. I knew God would save me as I fall to my knees confessing that though I am strong in some ways, I am really weak. I need Him as much where I think I am strong as where I know I am weak. It is only through His strength and His wisdom that I can see my way clear.

Journey of Faith 2007

Week of January 21

I must admit this week some despair has crept into my heart. Perhaps it's brought on in part by the continuous cold, wet, and rainy days that settled over this city. Or maybe the rise and fall, roller-coaster ride of Bill's blood counts has caused my emotional ups and downs. Maybe it is the result of my life taking a detour from the ordinary that pushes up those frightening thoughts. I wish suffering weren't a part of the landscape of life—so much uncertainty, so many questions, and sometimes so few answers. I wouldn't have chosen this path, but God reminds me that I must give Him all my despair and anxiety. Adversities in life are for God's glory and my good. The challenges that are beyond our control belong to Him.

As I lie in bed at night, my mind races, trying to figure out how all of this is going to turn out; it overwhelms me! At this point the sweet peace of God surrounds me with His love, reminding me to accept my finite understanding and to trust God's omnipotence. Hope then covers me like a blanket and sleep comes to my weary body. God takes away my despair, enabling me to see these ups and downs as a part of His larger plan. In Christ my hope is complete. God turns my despair to trust giving hope beyond comprehension. God is faithful, allowing me to see how He has chosen to use the difficult circumstances of life for His glory.

I know my sweet husband is dealing with many of his own emotions, but somehow in the mist of all these challenges, he continues to have an upbeat attitude around me. Bill, the patient, has actually become the caregiver of the caregiver. He is my inspiration and best supporter. He is not easily discouraged even through these days of hospitalization.

The little setbacks do not bother him because he uses them to embrace the promises of God. He truly lives out the Scripture verse, "This is the day the LORD has made; we will rejoice and be glad in it" (Ps. 118:24 NKJV).

Bill received an environmental promotion! His room was upgraded, allowing him to vacate the isolation room, moving to a regular room on this floor. However, the mask, gown, and glove rule is still in effect. The room has two large windows facing downtown Houston, with a spectacular view of the night lights. The banner from our church family, displayed on a wall, reminds us of their love.

Daily antibiotics continue to flow through Bill's body, fighting off the infection that lingers and stubbornly resists all efforts to eliminate it. Doctors express concern about his persistent cough and wheezing. Blood results on Monday indicated slight signs of cytomegalovirus (CMV), a common virus usually not harmful to people with normal immune systems. Many people have been infected with CMV without knowing it, showing no symptoms of being sick. This means the virus has become dormant (sleeping) in the body causing no ongoing or active infection. However, if the immune system becomes suppressed, such as after a bone-marrow/stem-cell transplant, the virus can reactivate (wake up) and start to cause problems with an active or ongoing infection. If the infection becomes widespread or affects vital organs, such as the lungs, it can be serious. Join me in praying that this virus will be eliminated from Bill's body. On Wednesday, Bill received another blood transfusion to help increase his red blood cell and hemoglobin counts. His energy level should have a boast, enabling us to walk a few more laps around this hospital floor.

I'm learning that all encounters with others are not by chance but for a purpose, especially when you pray for God to use you. God brings people and situations into my life for reasons that He alone knows. As I waited one evening in the hospital lobby for my ride back to the apartment, I sat reflecting on the events of the day. I cried as I thought about so many things, missing family and friends back home, concerns for Bill, and just feeling overwhelmed with the current lifestyle changes. Then I noticed tears streaming down the cheeks of a lady who sat down beside me. Our eyes met, and I reached out to her. For several seconds neither one of us could speak, but we understand each other, and our deep emotions brought a spirit of unity. Her husband, recovering from surgery, had a serious complication that could result in death. This lady was afraid, feeling alone and helpless.

As we shared together, we talked about when we are most afraid God's love calms us. He does this through his Word. "Do not be afraid, for I have ransomed you. I have called you by name; you are mine. When you go through deep waters, I will be with you. When you go through rivers of difficulty, you will not drown" (Isa. 43:1–2 NLT). Going through rivers of difficulty can either cause us to drown or help us to grow stronger. God will enable us to get through any situation, and sometimes He uses people we encounter to help us along the way. What joy filled my heart as my new friend and I shared phone numbers and hugged each other good-bye. Oh, the wonder of God's love!

On Thursday morning the rain has stopped, and the sun is shining brightly, reminding me of God's mercies that are new every morning. I'm learning to turn my eyes away from myself and keep them focused on His amazing grace.

We love each of you, our faithful prayer partners.

God knows all of my struggles and understands my heartaches, especially my concern as day after day I watch Bill's body labor to regain its strength during those hospitalization days. "O Lord, You have searched me and known me. You know my sitting down and my rising up; You understand my thought afar off. You comprehend my path and my lying down, and are acquainted with all my ways. For there is not a word on my tongue, but, behold, O Lord, You know it altogether" (Ps. 139:1–4 NKJV).

During those difficult days when Bill was so extremely ill, he also dealt with his own battles. Bill later recalled, "I felt I was near death's door. I was so sick at one point that I asked God to take me home." Bill is convinced that was the turning point for his recovery because after that incident his health slowly but steadily improved. I could relate to what Paul said in Philippians 2:27. "For indeed, he (Bill) was sick to the point of death. But God had mercy on him, and not on him only but also on me, so that I would not have sorrow upon sorrow".

God never gave me more than I could handle even though I thought at times He had and I was ready to fold up. Sometimes I was so overwhelmed by my life's situation that the crushing waves of disappointments, Bill's debilitating illness with all those setbacks were causing feelings of hopelessness, despair and even depression. I was mesmerized by the sight of terrifying darkness and the helpless desolation that I felt. But somehow God kept me going. He lovingly kept sustaining me through each of those dark, threatening rainstorms. When my faith was weak, and when the days of uncertainty became like stormy waves tossing from a hurricane's aftermath that just kept going on and on with no sign of relief that was when God would give me calmness with His peace. God wanted me to have faith and belief that He was right in the midst of any squall I might face. I often remembered those three words that Jesus spoke during a storm. He said, "It is I". Those words offered so much comfort, reassurance and hope that Jesus is enough. Jesus' presence is enough to stop the howling storm and calm the raging seas. Whatever my circumstances might be, Jesus is present with His love, compassion and grace. He can carry me safety through any trial that overwhelms me. I need to reach out to the Lord and trust His tender care. God's love does not keep me from trials it helps me get through them.

After weeks of stormy darken skies, God finally sent those first rays of sunlight, peeping through the clouds bringing a joyful step to my walk. The sight of the sun lancing through the clouds was like a pillar of hope appearing. Though the storm might continue to roll and shape my environment, still this was a sign that it would be over soon. I felt a powerful connection to that ray of sun. The sight gave me the encouragement that Bill and I would survive this storm. It would pass.

I often thought about that rainstorm that lasted forty days and forty nights. God opened the floodgates of heaven, and He let it rain. Those were dark days. How did Noah and his family feel as they went through that downpour? They probably had some of the same feelings I have had. But even more important, how did they feel when that first ray of sunshine hit the ark?

God walked me through some of the deepest waters imaginable during those post-transplant days, but the flood did not over take me. Behind those dark clouds the sun did shine lighting my pathway out of despair and helplessness. He became my shelter and shield, my ultimate protection, and my great refuge of hope. I was learning that to survive any storm, I would need to be anchored to the Rock of Ages.

Journey of Faith 2007

March 7,

I'm learning that the purpose of testing is to strengthen my character, deepening my trust in God and His perfect timing. When my trust begins to waiver and I become paralyzed with fear, I then remember all the great works of our Lord and His faithfulness to me. Through every step of this journey, God has demonstrated over and over that He is faithful and that I can access His help through faith and dependence on Him. His love has endured in each situation I have faced. He has promised to show me where to walk, and He has led me forward on a firm footing, even when

I have waivered. God is using daily experiences and challenges to get my attention so that He can restructure my priorities, shaping me into His likeness for the glory of His name.

CHAPTER 19

Making Progress
Reflections from the Journey, Days 25–40

The doctors are keeping a close eye for any signs of Bill's immune system rejecting the stem cells and also looking for any potentially deadly side effects from the graft-versus-host disease, Acute GVHD. Stem-cell-transplant patients can have various forms of GVHD and even find themselves battling chronic GVHD complications years after the transplant. Bill is receiving an immune-suppressant medication called Prograf to help prevent any acute forms of GVHD, which usually occurs in the first one hundred days after transplant. That is probably why patients are required to stay close to the hospital those one hundred days. The seriousness of GVHD can vary from mild to moderate, causing skin rashes or blistering, vomiting, or liver or lung damage. One of every five cases of acute GVHD can be life threatening.

One particularly dangerous form of GVHD ravages the stomach and intestines, causing unremitting vomiting and diarrhea. Usually the treatment plan to offset this type GVHD calls for super-high doses of the steroid prednisone for weeks to suppress out-of-control immune cells and inflammation. The side effects can be severe. Patients usually encounter infections. More steroids are then injected. Some patients will not improve; however, recent research studies are now testing treatments aimed at calming the GVHD problems without the steroid toxicity.

When someone receives a transplanted organ, such as a heart, the big fear is that their own immune system will attack the new heart and see it as foreign tissue. But with GVHD there is an opposite problem. It occurs when the donor's T cells, whose job is to hunt for the cancer cells and destroy them, becomes too aggressive and not only attacks the cancer cells but starts to attack the good cells as well. Graft-versus-host disease occurs when the new bone marrow (the graft) recognizes the tissues of patient's body (the host) as foreign and reacts against the body.

I have been told that the first sign of a successful transplant is an increase in the number of white blood cells, which are the cells that protect your body from infection. Bill's white counts have improved, and I begin to see his red blood cells and platelets growing in number also. With these early indications of progress, Bill is allowed to leave the hospital and his protective environment room. We go back to our apartment.

Because Bill is susceptible to infection, I try to enforce all of the special precautions needed in caring for Bill. Whenever he leaves the apartment, Bill wears a mask. He has to avoid large crowds of people, especially people who might be ill or who have been exposed to illness. For several weeks after leaving the hospital, we do not socialize with many people. We only leave the apartment when we have to return daily to the hospital for treatments.

Bill and I become very aware that the air we breathe, the food we eat, the hands we shake, as well as the items we touch have the potential for bacteria, viruses, or fungi that can cause infection. For a healthy individual these daily encounters with sources of infection are not a problem because normal, healthy immune systems protect most people from infections. But Bill's immune system can remain compromised for six months to a year after transplant, which requires taking necessary precautions.

Journey of Faith 2007

January 30,

Dear Family, Church Family, and Friends,
    Latest News: Bill got his "discharge papers" from the hospital. This day final came!
    When you look at the word *faith* and the word *wait*, both words have the letters ait. Someone once said that 60 percent (3/5) of faith is in the wait! Sometimes our faith needs to wait patiently for God's timetable. Waiting for God to help is not always an easy process, but there are benefits to be gained. The process reminds me of our grandchildren waiting for a cake to come out of the oven. Their impatient voices cry over and over, "Grandma, when is it going to be done? It's taking too long!" The thirty-five-minute bake time seems like forever to them. As they watch the oven window, the cake slowly rises to the top of the pan. I assure them it won't be long now. Their anticipation soon turns to great delight as they enjoy the benefit that came from the wait. "Grandma, you sure do make a good chocolate cake."

Sometimes life experiences require waiting patiently, and like little children we get impatient. It's taking too long! Sometimes the days of waiting for Bill's hospitalization stay to end was like waiting for a cake to bake without the oven on. It seemed like it was taking forever, twenty days to be exact! Waiting wasn't always easy, but God used those days for our benefit, showing us more about His loving care.

God carried us through anxious moments and steadied our faith. He allowed us to feel our deepest emotions, and He heard our cry as we waited, filling us with His joy and peace. The writer in Psalm 40:1–5 expressed it this way: in the wait time God can lift us out of our despair, setting our feet on solid ground. He will steady us as we walk, putting a new song of praise in our mouth. Often blessings cannot be received unless we go through the trials of waiting. "O Lord my God, you have performed many wonders for us. Your plans for us are too numerous to list" (Ps. 40:5 NLT).

The excitement of having Bill's white counts rise to 1.0 and not dip back down plus being able to return to our Houston apartment are just some of God's wonders! I can see hair starting to grow back on the top of Bill's head, fuzzy little peach hairs! These small increments of success gives us great hope, filling us with joy and gladness, knowing that sometimes realizing things that seem to take longer God will use for faith building.

Before leaving the hospital, we were required to participate in a discharge teaching session. The nurse instructor went over a packet of information including the do's and don'ts of living outside the hospital walls. I laughed as I watched my dear husband dose off throughout most of the instruction time. Bill could not keep his eyes open due to medication taken earlier for the removal of one of his CVC port lines. Instead of the three lines, he now has only two.

The nurse instructor would be speaking to Bill, and then his eyes would slowly close. She and I giggled as Bill tried hard to stay alert. He kept falling asleep. I even elbowed him several times, but it wasn't long before his eyes would shut again. After the nurse finished, I woke Bill up and told him he would not be receiving an A for this class! It's a good thing I was paying attention, or they might have reversed Bill's discharge papers! Bill will have to be careful to take the necessary precautions as we go back and forth to the hospital for daily treatments and checkups. He is required to wear a mask when we leave the apartment, avoid crowds, and especially wash his hands frequently.

Today was day 25 from transplant, one fourth of the way to that one-hundred-day milestone. As each day is marked off on our wall calendar, I praise God and thank Him continually for the life-giving light of His presence during these days. He has faithfully answered our prayers with awesome deeds.

Our Love and Gratitude,
Bill and Barbara

Journey of Faith 2007

February 5,

Dear Family, Church Family, and Friends,

Before I give you an update, I want our church family to know how special it was for Bill to talk with you during the Sunday morning services. We watched the time, eagerly waiting for 10:45. I'm thankful that we have phones connecting us together. We felted the love and warmth of being with you. I told Bill to start preparing an Easter message because I believe the Lord will make it possible for us to be in Lawrenceburg that Sunday. The one hundred days are not over until April 15, but we all know God's time frame and plans may be different.

Our daily routine has changed now that Bill is an outpatient. We spend the early mornings in our apartment. Around 11:00 a.m. I drop Bill off at the hospital where he spends five to six hours receiving his intravenous therapy treatments. His first stop is the Diagnostic Center where his blood is drawn. Then he reports to the Stem Cell Transplant Ambulatory Treatment Center (ACT) where he is placed in a room.

Depending on the results of the lab report, he could be given several intravenous supplements. His progress is carefully monitored for any signs of infection or graft-versus-host disease (GVHD). A BMT clinical nurse specialist examines Bill daily and has assured us that Bill is making progress. Our assigned pharmacist reviews Bill's medications, assisting with any necessary changes, and is available to answer any questions. Bill's primary doctor sees him on Tuesday.

This new schedule allows me to have more personal time because I don't need to stay with Bill while he is in the ACT Center. In fact ACT staff encourages caregivers to use this time for themselves. Once I have dropped Bill off for the day, I have time to work on some projects, run some errands, do laundry, clean our two-room apartment, or just relax with a book. I usually walk to the hospital to check on Bill and then walk back to the apartment. Our apartment is about a mile from the hospital so walking is great exercise. When Bill completes his daily treatments, he calls for his personal chauffeur, and I bring him back to our apartment. Bill is usually tried after the day so we just relax in our Houston home during the evening hours.

As Bill continues to improve, his daily hospital trips will transition to just several visits a week, giving us more free time. The first free day we plan to get in our car and drive around Houston. A change of scenery will be refreshing for Bill. Would you believe we have not put gas in our car since December 18, last year! What a change because I usually have to fill my gas tank at least two or more times each week going back and forth to work.

Bill still experiences nausea and can only tolerate small portions of food. His weight is stable between 170 and 173 pounds. I have started doing some baking, so as Bill's appetite increases, hopefully he can add a few more pounds. His energy level is low, requiring frequent naps during the day. He will start physical therapy this week, which should increase mobility and tone up his muscles.

M. D. Anderson has several programs for caregivers. This past Wednesday I went to a support group for transplant-patient caregivers. This group consisted of four wives with husbands as patients and three mothers with children in their twenties, plus two social workers and one chaplain. I listened mostly as one by one the ladies shared her concerns and feelings about how cancer had impacted their lives. Words of encouragement and hugs were generously given. These are hard times for many people as they cope with many stresses. One wife was in tears as she told us she had just found out that her husband who was on day 98 will have to stay longer due to complications.

I listened as they shared stories about their struggles. One husband was on his third stem-cell transplant and weighs only 117 pounds. We were total strangers, but our common situations bonded us together. My heart hurt for one lady who expressed many doubts and had little hope that her life could be better. She was so bitter that cancer had taken so much from her. Maybe in time I can share with her the hope we have in Christ Jesus.

I find my most comfort when I recall how God has worked in the past. My great God who parted the Red Sea, an incredible miracle, provided a pathway that no one knew was there. I know that God is capable, trustworthy, and will lead me along this journey, showing me a pathway that I may not see at first glance, but the pathway is there! I have found great comfort in God's sustaining power through difficulties. I put aside those doubts about how this transplant is going to turn out, and I begin to worship God and His holiness. "You are the God of great wonders! You demonstrate your awesome power among the nations" (Ps. 77:14 NLT). My confidence and security are in this great God, and I will cling to Him and trust His pathways.

Bill's 30-day tests will take place tomorrow, Tuesday. We have to be at the hospital at 6:00 a.m., and according to our schedule our last appointment is at 6:00 p.m. The long day will consist of a complete PET Lymphoma Restage, chest, PA & LAT, blood/specimen collection, bone marrow aspiration, and intravenous therapy. The test results will reveal how the new cells are growing, which is the first sign of a successful transplant.

> Yet I still belong to you; you hold my right hand. You guide me with your counsel, leading me to a glorious destiny (Ps. 73:23–24 NLT).

I'm confident God knows our daily situation and that He cares. He is the Light of each new day!

Love,
Bill and Barbara

Journey of Faith 2007

February 11,

Bill has better days and then some that are not as great. The nausea is a real problem so the doctors have scheduled an EGD with biopsy to make sure that he does not have GVHD symptoms in the stomach. All the test results from last week have not been given to us. We will meet with Bill's stem-cell doctor this week for that consultation. Bill's white blood cells were 1.6 this past Friday. Bill was given a blood transfusion last Wednesday, so his energy level did increase. This is a slow, day-to-day process, but we are definitely seeing improvement. Keep praying for Bill's total recovery. I know that God is working in his healing process, and He is also teaching me many things as well.

Before we came to M. D. Anderson, we received a packet in the mail giving us several maps for guiding us not only around the Houston area but also a campus map for the Texas Medical Center, which is composed of M. D. Anderson as well other hospitals. The Texas Medical Center claims to be one of the largest having some forty-five institutions. Having now spent these days here, I do feel somewhat comfortable knowing my way around the cancer hospital. The hospital is like a little city with large food courts, several cafes, bakery shops, gift stores, beauty/barber shop, hospitality centers, learning centers, chapels, patient education classrooms, and hotels that connect to the hospital.

The cancer center uses sky bridges to connect several of its large buildings. Golf cart rides are provided for patients who are unable to walk. Elevators are designated by a letter. So if you want to go to the Leukemia Center, the direction would say Main Building, elevator A, floor 8. The hospital also designed landmarks to guide people to certain destinations. People can find their way around, and they don't get lost. For example, a picture of a fish indicates that you are in The Aquarium section of the hospital; a picture of tree indicates The Tree Sculpture section; an art picture indicates The Art Gallery; and a gazebo indicates The Gazebo, and so forth. It is an amazing complex as you follow the access pathway, marked with blue Access signs and carpet stripes to the various landmarks. When you arrive at the landmark, you use the maps and signs to find your exact destination.

The landmark that continues to remind me of a greater landmark is the picture of a fountain indicating The Fountain section of the hospital. This section is the beautiful, four-story main lobby with a large, magnificent fountain of water cascading up and down in the center. This is the lobby I walk through to get to Bill's hospital room. Over the front door of the lobby is the sign "Welcome to the Fountain." How appropriate that the main hospital entrance is called "The Fountain." Many people enter through "The Fountain" hospital doors thirsting for the cleansing healing solutions from the cancer that has consumed their bodies. There is another picture of a fountain that I have been reminded of as I have sat in that lobby. In God's Holy Word the "fountain of life" (Ps. 36:9) is a vivid image of fresh, cleansing water that gives life to the spiritually thirsty. God is called the fountain of the living water. Jesus spoke of Himself as living water that could quench thirst forever and give eternal life. That landmark sign reads, "Welcome to My Fountain" where there is living water, a never-ending stream flowing from the throne of grace supplying us with God's mercy, forgiveness, and cleansing power. "With joy you will drink deeply from the fountain of salvation!" (Isa. 12:3 NLT). This fountain will give access to the pathway to eternal life in Jesus Christ. If you follow that pathway, the greatest healing of all occurs. That joy satisfies completely.

We send our love to all of you, and may each day you know what a blessing you are to God's kingdom. You have certainly blessed our lives.

Bill and Barbara

Journey of Faith 2007

February 14,

When there is good news, you just have to share it. From the preliminary test reports, Bill's doctors were pleased, repeatedly saying that everything looks good! The stem cells are reproducing. Praise the Lord for these visible signs that God is healing and restoring Bill's body with new blood cells. Bill turned a major corner in this journey on day 37. He started to feel stronger, and for the past two days he has had no nausea, actually eating three meals a day without any side effects. We know there will be more corners to turn in the days ahead, but each experience brings us closer to our ultimate destination.

Traveling down this journey, we often do not know what is around each corner until we turn to face it. When Bill was diagnosed with cancer eight years ago, I couldn't believe it. No one ever thinks it will happen to them, but it does. Someone said, "Life is never the same again. It's like moving into a different dimension of living—this "cancer world," and no one truly understands what it is like until they have experienced it themselves." I remember those first new days when we walked the halls of MDA hospital. My eyes met the eyes of others walking the halls. There was an acknowledgment, a knowing look, a kindred fellowship, a bond we all shared. We were all fighting cancer together no matter whether we were rich or poor, kings or paupers, black, brown or white. Cancer is the great leveler of us all. We can put our arms around strangers and comfort them when they are discouraged or grieving. We can laugh with them when they need a break from the seriousness of life. We can extend a hand when someone needs help. And we can listen when someone needs to talk. What a special place this is. I know we are here for a divine reason.

God helps me appreciate each day and to be grateful every day that we live. Life is truly a gift. Never take life for granted, and never miss a day without telling those closest to you how much you love them or how much you appreciate them. Bill and I want to express to you our love and appreciation for the bond of love we share together. Your prayers on our behalf have been heard, and our lives have been touched by your commitment to pray daily for us. Your love has been demonstrated to us in so many ways. The daily mail of cards and e-mails, the care packages, and the phone calls have meant so much to us. Our church family continues to support us during this journey, and they have helped us survive some of the financial and logistical burdens of having cancer. We have no concerns about our finances. Ladies of the church have sent me so many treasured love gifts. They have pampered me with body lotions, devotional books, candy, homemade breads, videos, and so many gifts that I can't begin to list them all. Thank you for your love and encouragement. You have offered us help at just the right moments, when it was needed the most. Our gratitude humbles us, and we thank our Lord for each of you and the blessings you are to us.

With this being Valentine's Day, we especially wanted to tell you how much we love you. If we could see you in person, we would hug you and let you know what this bond of love means to us.

Love,
Bill and Barbara

CHAPTER 20

Help, I'm a Caregiver!

My desire and heartfelt commitment to care for my husband has never wavered. Bill and I were in this journey together, and I would be there to support, love, and care for him through the entire transplant process. By signing my name on the caregiver form, I was acknowledging that I had read and understood my role as Bill's caregiver. M. D. Anderson requires all transplant patients to have a responsible adult who will be available twenty-four hours a day, seven days a week before the patient is admitted to the hospital for transplant. Because the experience of a stem-cell transplant is so complex and challenging for a patient, it is necessary to have someone available as a caregiver to support the patient not only during the transplant but also the months after the transplant.

According to the transplant manual, being a caregiver is a full-time job. It listed six main responsibilities. The first three required me to transport Bill to the hospital for appointments every day for at least fourteen weeks or one hundred days after receiving the transplant; make sure Bill was able to eat, drink, and sleep; give Bill his medications as instructed; and document his fatigue level. I felt confident I could do those tasks. The last three seemed rather easy as well, ensuring that Bill maintains adequate hygiene, immediately bringing Bill to the hospital in the case of an emergency, and providing updates to family and friends back home.

Members of the medical team had stated that I needed to notify them of any changes in Bill's condition such as fever, chills, vomiting, diarrhea, eating or drinking difficulties. They told me failure to notify the team of changes could seriously affect the outcome of the transplant.

Looking over the list of expectations, I felt certain I could do those six jobs, but soon my lack of nursing skills necessitated learning a few tools of the trade like how to give heparin injections, change the heparin cap, and change the dressing on the central venous catheter. I immediately enrolled in a couple of the required caregiver classes. I began practicing my newly acquired skills on patient Bill, always with a nurse looking over my shoulder.

As soon as I could demonstrate my competencies, a nurse signed the official slip of paper indicating I could pick up my nursing supplies at the hospital pharmacy. I was now able to perform these skills without the assistance of a real nurse. Having passed my Nursing 101 skill level test, I proudly accepted my bag of supplies.

The first time I went solo, I must admit to you, I experienced real panic, and so did Bill. His emotions were more like fear. I'm sure Bill thought, *My care is in the hands of this nurse caregiver, and she is having difficulty with this rather simple procedure. What's going to happen when it gets more complicated?* I had tried to give Bill his heparin injection, but the medicine would not go through the line. I knew I had connected the syringe to the injection cap so I couldn't figure why it wasn't working. Remembering the nurse's instructions, "Do not force the heparin if resistance is met," I slowly tried to inject the heparin. The syringe appeared to be stuck. I did not want to take Bill back to the hospital, especially having to admit my deficiencies as his caregiver so I quickly called my new friend, Ramie. She was the caregiver for her son, Tyler, who at that time was thirty-one days post transplant. They were staying in one of the downstairs apartments. I knew she could show me what to do. Ramie heard my apprehensive, uneasy voice, "I need help." Both Ramie and Tyler came to my rescue. Tyler simply pushed down on the plunger, and the solution went right into the line on the first try. Bill didn't say anything, but I knew he was thinking that perhaps I needed to repeat my Nursing 101 class.

As the days passed, my confidence level did increase, in spite of that first experience with the heparin injection. I had stored the nursing supplies in the bathroom linen closet and lined up Bill's medicines on the top of one of the bedroom dresser drawers, which served as my apartment pharmacy. Keeping track of the times Bill took his medicines became a daily task. I faithfully recorded each pill going into my patient's mouth. Several times a day I took Bill's temperature, and I monitored his food intake. I encouraged Bill to be as independent as possible, allowing him to resume normal activities as tolerated.

The medical team helped me understand about possible changes in Bill's health and also the reality that there could be complications. How I responded would be critical. It would be important to remain positive, helpful, and maintain a nonanxious presence in the midst of any crises. Those crises did come. Bill vomited. He developed a red rash on his body. Bill lost his appetite due to the constant state of being nauseated. He dropped weight, often dramatically. He frequently had sleepless nights and diarrhea. He needed IV fluids to rehydrate. Bill became moody, tried, and forgetful. He felt so weak I had to push him in a wheelchair. His blood counts dropped, making his blood chemistry levels severely imbalanced. He needed blood transfusions.

Sometimes I remained calm; other times the shock at how poorly I thought Bill was doing make my adrenaline pump up so much I could feel an anxiety attack approaching.

Handling the many tasks and situations I faced was physically challenging and emotionally draining. The rigors of giving care were ongoing and frightening. Watching Bill undergo those difficult medical procedures was taxing to me. Sometimes my sheer exhaustion and doubts kept me wondering, *I'm not sure I can do all of this.* During one of those moments I recalled a book my grandchildren loved for me to read, the timeless classic *The Little Engine That Could.* That determined little train climbed the steep hill by chanting positively, "I think I can, I think I can, I think I can." The little engine faced an uphill climb that seems insurmountable. And then, as if gained more resolve, it declared "I know I can. I know I can.," which we all know resulted in his getting to the top of the hill. In reading that story, I see a can-do, positive attitude throughout the book. When I am faced with situations or circumstances that appear impossible, I begin to program my mind into believing I can do this. I can handle these caregiving responsibilities. I can and I will do this!

Continually repeating positive thoughts until they sink into my mind got me through many of those caregiver's experiences. In fact those "I think I can" moments and my ability to laugh at myself might just have been the push I needed to advance me the level of Nursing 102.

Here's an experience I won't forget!

Journey of Faith 2007

February 11,

I never would have signed up for a nursing class in college. It was just not the field I wanted to study, but oh my, now do I ever wish I had! This past week Bill had his first days off from making the daily trips to the clinic. I was given the instructions on how to administer the intravenous therapy from the apartment. I felt comfortable after the nurse went through the ten-minute training session, with four sheets of written instruction. I can surely do this. I do know how to read.

I assured the nurse Bill would get his IV treatments. Feeling confident, I put my signature on the sign-out sheet for the portable infusion pump and walked out of the hospital with a large bag filled with the supplies needed. The next day, nurse Barbara, with instructions nearby, followed the step-by-step procedures. I had the IV bag ready with tubing primed (that means that I had pushed and pushed the bag of medication so that it is now in the tubing.) Oh, I forgot to tell you. I first washed my hands, put on my gloves, prepared a workspace, and have taken the bag out of the refrigerator for at least two hours prior. I sure don't want cold medication going through my husband's veins, especially since his IV port is near his heart. I don't want the preacher to have a cold heart. I'm sure our church family appreciates that!

The next step was to install the new cassette in the pump. The pump has been programmed for continuous infusion, allowing the delivery of the specified amount of fluid over a three-hour time period at a specific rate of flow. I heard the two clicks as the cassette was placed in the pump and the four latches were holding the cassette securely in its pocket. I then placed the tubing in the tubing channel, flushed Bill's IV catheter, and connected the tubing to it. Oh, I did make sure that the catheter clamp was opened! Next I turned the pump on by pressing the on/off button. The pump went through its self-test mode, and I was feeling more confident as the minutes went by. I pushed the ENTER button when the screen says USING BATTERIES, then pressed 1 and followed the arrows until I heard the little pump beeping. It's working! What a cute little beeping sound! Not quiet as loud as the ones used in the hospital.

Having accomplished hooking up my husbands IV infusion for the day, I proudly sat down to gloat in my accomplishment. Needing to be humbled somewhat, I panicked when I could no longer hear the beeping sound. I tried desperately to fix the problem. Machines have never been my forte. I soon was ready to toss it in the trash, except it is now connected to my husband. To make a long story short, I ended up walking to the hospital carrying the tote bag filled with Bill's bag of fluid, the IV tubing, and the portable infusion pump. I left Bill at the apartment. The "real" nurses were very helpful. That's all I need to say about this experience!

I'm so thankful God cares, loves, and guides me, even when I do stupid things and make mistakes. One time I gave Bill the wrong medicine. I felt so bad, but the nurse assured me Bill would be alright. I realized over and over I could not be the caregiver I need to be in my own strength. Many of the tasks were difficult. But by the grace of God, He gave me the power and strength I needed. I claimed the promised of John 15:5, "I am the vine; you are the branches. If a man remains in me and I in him, he will bear much fruit; apart from me you can do nothing."

God helps me to have a clear head, an upbeat, happy attitude, for I know that is important. I sometimes feel exhausted, frustrated, and even annoyed at Bill. I get tired of the hospital routine, the disease, and the treatments. I ask myself many times, "What does my demeanor convey to Bill?" My attitude can have an effect on Bill. I cannot raise my loved one's spirits any higher than my own spirits are raised. Shifting my focus from the negative to the positive helps me get through those difficult times.

A good friend told me happy people know there are silver linings in every dark cloud and that lessons will be learned and wisdom gained from every experience. Happiness and joy are choices I can make, and I am deciding to find them in each challenge that comes my way. During these months of Bill's recovery, I am striving to have a positive, optimistic attitude because I know that will be infectious and can be a major factor in the success of my husband's transplant. However, there are times I must admit it is hard to practice.

I believe it's sometimes more trying on the well person than the sick person. I feel so helpless standing by, for I want to do more. I often feel powerless to change a situation. I cannot stop Bill's pain or cure the disease or predict the future. The increased responsibilities, plus the emotional stress are piling up in my mind. I think about the treatment procedures and outcomes often. How will Bill react to this medicine? Will he need another transfusion this week? These are just a few of the things that linger in my thoughts. Also the feelings of fear and anxiety that go with having a loved one with a life-threatening illness are like an ever-present baggage that hangs on my shoulders. The load gets heavy at times. There is always the real possibility I will be left behind. Trying to stay positive for Bill and meanwhile trying to deal with the negative thoughts swirling in my mind become a challenge.

I quickly see I cannot help Bill if I am overwhelmed, strained, or burned out. I know I need to stay in good shape, stay healthy, and keep my mind positive. So in order to maintain my ability to cope mentally and emotionally with the day-to-day experiences, I need to implement some coping strategies. I also realize I do not need to pretend to be OK when I am not. I allow myself to cry. If I keep stuffing those anxious emotions deep down inside me, they would only find unhealthy ways to come out later on. I know if I do not deal with them, they will deal with me. So talking about my feelings and taking steps to care for myself are the keys to handling my stress, enabling me to be more in control of my emotions plus energizing me physically.

Caregivers need to have our batteries recharged probably a lot more often than we want to admit, but how do we do that? Here are some things I am trying. I attempt to have a balance in my routine by finding ways to relax and take breaks from caregiving. I make time to do something for myself.

During Bill's long hospital stay, I took walks outside just to get away from the hospital environment. The sunshine and fresh air give me time out so I can temporarily disengage from my thoughts and feelings, especially stressful ones. When the weather becomes inclement, I exercise by walking through the hospital halls. Walking back and forth to the hospital becomes a great way to take a break. I sometimes talk to myself, sing a hymn, or reflect on Scripture verses. Walking decreased my stress, and it boosted my energy.

I try to eat three nutritious meals each day. Sometimes I will stay in Bill's hospital room and just order food off the guest menu. Other times I'll walk to the hospital cafeteria. I make sure I get plenty of rest and sleep, and faithfully take my vitamins. I know Bill needs to be around a healthy caregiver due to his suppressed immune system so I'm cautious to avoid sick people. If I get worn out physically and were to contract a respiratory problem, this could jeopardize Bill's recovery.

Working crossword puzzles and playing board games are especially engaging and fun. Bill and I pass the time with these during the months of recovery. I love to read, so I spend time catching up on some of my favorite authors. Someone mailed us several good joke books that keep us laughing and finding the humor in life. We found that laughing together, especially over life's little twists and turns, is a wonderful way to let off pressures and keep stress at a minimum. I guess that's why Bill and I enjoy watching funny movies. We would laugh until we were silly.

I had heard scientists believe that, even though humor cannot cure disease, it has profound physical and psychological benefits. Laughter strengthens the immune system. When a person has a really good laugh, the body produces more immunoglobulin A, the body's warrior against upper respiratory infections. Laughter is not only good for the body; it's good for the soul. I have given myself permission to laugh at myself and at the stupid things I sometimes do as Bill's caregiver. These moments of laughter nourish my spirit and remind me it's all right to laugh. I believe God even laughs with me.

Music can be uplifting so each morning I play some of Bill's favorite CDs as we prepare for the day. We both have our quiet times and then those moments together where we can share what God has revealed in His Word. Bill and I talk about life, the present and the past. Our yesterdays are treasures from the past to be cherished and enjoyed again and again. We talk about what great fun memories we have and all the fun trips we are going on once Bill is well. We relive those moments by looking through our family album. Our apartment bedroom doors are covered with pictures of our children, grandchildren, and church family. Just having their pictures in view gives us the feeling they are close by and helps us remember their love for us.

Keeping busy with things I enjoy doing enables me to adjust to my new environment and circumstances. I spend time each day writing journal entries to my unborn grandchild. I also keep my mind engaged by working on a job-related project that I brought. I'm developing several chapters for an infant and toddler training manual. These personal, pleasurable tasks have become a diversion from my caregiving duties.

What I enjoy most is the additional time I have to spend in God's Word. I'm taking advantage of the slower pace to analyze what is truly important. God is giving me time to "be still." "Be still, and know that I am God" (Ps. 46:10). These quiet times are refreshing me and giving me new opportunities to review the many fundamental truths that are frequently overlooked because back home my schedule had become so busy that I found myself always rushing through God's Word, not having the time to meditate and absorb God's holiness.

His Word is my comfort and strength, especially as I read through the Psalms. The psalmists had plenty of trouble in their lives, plenty of times they desperately needed God's help. I know that one reason I love reading the Psalms is because they speak about what I'm experiencing. Seeing God's faithfulness and goodness gives me the encouragement to keep on going and not faint or give up.

God knew there would be many heartaches involved in caring for a loved one so that is why He gave me such great comfort from His Word. He also knew the separation from my family and friends would be hard, so making new friends lessened my sense of isolation. I'm getting emotional support from several other transplant caregivers that I have met through the hospital support groups. I'm not alone in my struggles as other caregivers share similar experiences including the highs and lows, the laughter and the heartaches. We are like one big family that has been united in a kindred spirit of togetherness. Having this kind of support is a critical component to the caregiving equation. It makes being a caregiver a lot easier.

CHAPTER 21

Circumstances Become Opportunities for Ministries

The Scriptures teach about a God who "redeems [my] life from the pit," who satisfies my desires with "good things" so that I am "renewed like the eagle" (Ps. 103:4–5). Some of the good things out of our circumstances were the people Bill and I were connecting with whom we might not ever have met if it were not for the situations God was allowing us to experience. God brought people into our lives that lifted our spirits, made us smile, and encouraged us with words and acts of kindness. Not only did we receive many blessings during our Houston stay, but God also opened up doors of opportunities for us.

Opportunities come in all shapes and sizes. God started bringing people into my life and providing many occasions for me to meet other caregivers and patients. Because of our similar experiences, a unique bond instantaneously connected us. People felt open to talk freely about their medical experiences because everyone could identify and understand. The comparable feelings and struggles were easy to share. Cancer has a funny way of putting everybody on equal ground. It doesn't matter if you're rich or poor, college educated or a high school dropout, or if you are living in a mansion or a shack. Anybody can get cancer.

I remember the first day we rode the shuttle from our apartment to the hospital. Before I could plop down in my seat, I quickly scanned the other people on the bus. Four couples were scattered about the bus. I quickly recognized who the patients and the caregivers were, for each carried a certain look on their faces. The patients appeared frail, and the caregivers looked scared and tired. Behind each expression is a story. Some faces disclosed hopelessness, communicating, "I don't know how much more I can handle." The pain goes beyond the bounds of medicine. I wanted to reach out to them and say, "Yes, you are right. You cannot bear this on your own, but I know a personal God who has said, "It's not too much for Me." God can truly meet all of our needs.

I nodded my head as I exchanged a greeting, finding a seat beside my patient. Soon more conversation follows. Where are you from? What kind of cancer do you have? It is easy for the people to talk because we are all fighting cancer. We are all involved in individual skirmishes, combating the same enemy.

Journey of Faith 2007

March 7,

I'm rejoicing not only in God's care but also in how He has placed people in our paths while we are here in Houston. Bill and I have had opportunities to meet many people. We have been able to share our faith and talk with them about their own battles and personal struggles with cancer. One patient living in the apartment across from us died, and we visited with his wife, showing our support and love. Bill met a young Christian medical staff member whom he mentors weekly.

I have met two special friends, one a mom from Wyoming and the other a mom from Mississippi. Both of these ladies are caregivers for their sons: Scott, 26, and Tyler, 19. Their testimony of faith and courage as they support their children during their cancer journeys has given me fresh insights into how God uses even our children to teach us more of His faithfulness and grace.

Mrs. Williams, a beautiful lady of ninety years, is undergoing chemo treatments and daily manages the stairs to her second-floor apartment. She will undergo surgery as soon as her cancer is under control. She always has a smile and a word of encouragement. Last Saturday we had our first couple over for dinner at our apartment. Boots' husband Lee is finishing up his twentieth radiation treatment. Connecting with people has given us opportunities for fellowshipping and has reduced the homesickness we feel being absent from our family and friends.

One thing I know for sure is that cancer has a way of making me a more compassionate and caring person. I really believe one of the elements of dealing with adversities is to turn eyes away from myself and look for those opportunities to respond to others. God used the story of Joseph in the Bible to teach me about ministries. Joseph was in a position to help others while he was in the dungeon because he was not sitting in a corner having a private pity party. He could have said, "Look, I've got my own problems."

But instead he reached out to help others. Joseph was sensitive to the hurts of those around him. He used his gifts and circumstances while living in a prison for opportunities to help those in need. I do not need to walk around with a long face. My Lord certainly takes away the gloom as I see all the blessings that come from meeting people and allowing God to use my circumstances for opportunities for ministry. Oh, Lord, help me to use each opportunity to rally around people, lending them a hand and pointing them to Jesus Christ.

Sour is definitely not a word to describe Bill because he is one of the most cheerful, optimistic persons I know. I can always count on him to give me a much-needed boost and even a laugh. Not only does he bring a smile to my face, but he also uses his buoyant outlook toward life as a way to minister to people. Bill is always ready to lend a hand to whoever needs help and he is never at a loss for words, especially when it comes to meeting new people. As we sit in a waiting room, I pick up a dog-eared magazine while my husband begins a conversation with the person seated next to him. Before leaving, Bill is scribbling off a note to exchange names and phone numbers. Bill and I can be classified as people persons. You might say we are usually considered as extroverts. People energize us and do not drain us.

I will forever be grateful for how God arranged that first-time meeting with Eric Thomas, another stem-cell transplant patient. It was a divine appointment. Now a divine appointment is one of those meetings God arranges at just the right time and place so He can show His power in someone's life. Sitting in the waiting area of the ATC (Ambulatory Treatment Center) is a common routine of all transplant patients. During this time you begin to learn names and develop acquaintances with those dealing with similar maladies as yourself. During one of those times, Eric's mother, Donna Thomas, approached Bill and asked if he were a minister. She had noticed Bill was carrying a Bible. He acknowledged that he was, and she began to tell Bill about her son, Eric. She had great concerns about his health. She would be returning to Las Vegas, the next day, and she asked Bill if he would check on Eric. Bill assured her he would be happy to do so and followed up by meeting Eric later that day.

From the first introduction Bill and Eric seemed to hit it off. Their schedules were not always the same, but when they were in the ATC area at the same time, they would visit. Within a few days Eric's fiancé, Kari, showed up in Bill's treatment room to introduce herself to him and to express her appreciation for his ministering to Eric. It wasn't long before we became friends with this couple and discovered that Eric was a young spinal surgeon from Albuquerque, New Mexico, who also traveled nationally as a medical teacher. Besides his private practice, Eric worked for a company called

NuVasive, a spinal hardware company where Eric is known by his friends as ET. Eric teaches other surgeons how to do spinal surgery, pioneering new techniques and methods for invasive spinal surgery. He had spent time in Brazil training doctors on these new techniques.

Eric had been diagnosed with a childhood form of leukemia the previous summer and had started his treatment at M. D. Anderson a couple of weeks before we arrived. He had received an unrelated stem-cell transplant on February 13, 2007. During the weeks and months of recovery, we spent time with this couple. Our fellowship was unique, and there was no doubt God was sovereignly working out His plans. Some good things were coming out of this cancer and transplant process. God had something special in store for both Bill and Eric. I saw how their relationship grew and how God used it to change Eric's life. Blessings can come when God and cancer meet. You will read later in the book about more of those blessings.

The ATC area became a good place for meeting stem-cell patients like Eric, as well as caregivers and staff at MDA. Because Bill had to spend many hours receiving treatments in that section of the hospital, he used some of his time to read. Bill has never been a TV watcher, so he carried his Bible and other books with him each day. Unaware of what others were thinking, Bill later was informed that he was known as "the man with his Bible." The Lord used his example to open numerous doors to share the gospel and to minister to others.

Early in Bill's visits to the ATC area, he met one of the receptionists. Every time he checked in, he exchanged conversation with her, and she soon learned that Bill was a pastor. About the third week of Bill's treatments, she began coming into his room, asking questions about the Bible and things of a spiritual nature. She showed a deep hunger for truth. This soon turned into a regular mentoring session in which various subjects of the Scriptures were discussed and explained. Her countenance and life began revealing a joy and happiness that filled the room when she walked in. She not only continued to ask questions but also shared perceptive insights about Scripture verses she was reading. What a blessing to see God create and feed a spiritual hunger in the heart of this young lady.

Later that year (August 2007) after we had returned to Tennessee, this lady sent this e-mail expressing her gratitude to Bill for the time he had spent with her.

Thank you soooo much, Mr. Betts. You will never know the impact you have made in my life. When I had lost hope and had almost given up on our men and women of God, then God sent you to M. D. Anderson just to show me hope. Thank you for

having a shepherd's heart. I will always cherish the time you took to answer all my questions and to challenge me to go deeper in the Word of God. Your seed was planted, and now I am a result of your ministry. Thank you for you and your wife's wisdom and encouragement. May God continue to bless you and your ministry exceedingly and abundantly.

I saw over and over how the providence of God was directing my steps by bringing people into my life. As soon as I met Ramie, I knew we were going to be friends. Her big smile welcomed Bill and me when we moved into our apartment. "Let me help you with those boxes," she said, as we unloaded the car settling into our Houston home. Ramie, an incredibly kind and caring person, was continually looking for ways to help people. She had arrived in Houston in November with her son, Tyler. When I met both of them, Tyler was on day 30 of his stem-cell transplant. Tyler's first year of college had been abruptly interrupted with a diagnosis of leukemia that was not responding well to traditional treatment plans. His positive attitude along with his grin made you an instant friend. Tyler was an inspiration to be around, for he never complained in spite of all the setbacks he encountered. He loved the Lord and looked forward to being in church, even when he had to wear the mask to protect his immune system from airborne viruses.

Both mother and son gave an amazing emotional and spiritual encouragement to everyone they met. I could easily talk with Ramie. We shared our caregiving concerns and stories. We also spent time together as we participated in a ladies Bible study that met for several weeks at a local church. Ramie told me about the cancer support meetings for caregivers. I found that I was not alone. Many caregivers were experiencing what I was going through. When the floodwaters of the storms come up to your inner being, you don't need challenges; you need the comfort of a friend who will come alongside and say, "I am hurting with you. I understand. I am here for you. Together we will get through this storm." Ramie and others became those friends.

One of the blessings of this life is getting to meet those Christian friends, and hopefully, our paths will continue to cross throughout our journeys until we finally meet in Immanuel's land, never to part. I am thankful God changed my priorities, allowing me to focus more on ministry than before. He helped me to see that in each new circumstance I would have opportunities for sharing and relating to people. Next to my eternal purpose of glorifying God and enjoying Him forever, I am saved by the grace of God through the cross of Christ so that I can tell others of His saving grace that they too may receive the gift of eternal life.

CHAPTER 22

Finding Peace in the Storm
Reflections from the Journey, Day 46

The song "Precious Lord, Take My Hand", and its sweet melody became my prayer for my mother as she struggled with the last months of her life. Its beautiful words of comfort wedged its way into my heart.

Mother was in tremendous pain, and she even asked me to pray that the Lord would take her home. As my mother's life was fading, I would have to come to grips with the physical loss as well. The song spoke of hope when I felt so helpless and gave voice to my hurting heart that often could find no words of its own. No matter what the storm or the night holds, God leads me on to the Light. He is holding my hand, helping me find peace in the storm.

Resting my head against the small window, I feel relieved no one sits beside me on the airplane, for I need the silence and the time to try to understand my feelings. I close my eyes reflecting on the many thoughts running through my mind. *Lord, times like this cause me to think about how much I need You. I thought I had everything under control. Bill's recovery has progressed well, just as we prayed. But now, my mom is dying. I knew her body would not last forever. Emotionally, I am not ready to say good-bye to her. Give me the strength to accept this.* My tears well up behind my eyelids, and I feel the knots gripping my stomach as I think about my mother. Over the years we have had our moments of tension. We did not always agree on everything, but she has been the mother God planned for me to have. I will forever respect her and be grateful for her influence.

Mother has been in a great deal of anguish since she fell on New Year's Eve. Her mind continues to be tormented with outbursts of dementia and stubbornness. Her suffering has broken my heart as her body has continued to deteriorate over these past months. I felt so helpless not being able to be with her. I prayed for the presence of God to overwhelm mom as she struggled between life and death. At times mom wanted to stay longer on this earth, but then sometimes she would say, "I'm ready to leave. Pray that I go to heaven soon. I want to die."

My sister, Peggy, became my mother's caregiver, overseeing Mother's escalating needs and all of the many health challenges that seemed to be spiraling downward. Mother had been moved from an assisted living center, to the hospital, to a rehabilitation center, to a nursing home, and now back to her assisted living apartment where she will remain until God calls her home. Peggy has kept me informed of mom's declining health. She tends to our mother's demanding daily needs. As we talk by phone and compare caregiver notes, I know my sister has a much tougher job. She faithfully cares for mother, sometimes day and night.

Today is Tuesday, day 46 of post transplant. Having made it through the initial difficult days, Bill has almost reached the halfway mark of the one hundred days. His hospital outpatient schedule has slowed down, allowing him to have a few days of receiving treatments at our apartment. My sister called early this morning. "Barbara, you need to come. Mom is not responding, and the hospice staff has informed me that mom will probably not make it through the day. It is only a manner of hours before her heart gives out. Her death is imminent." I quickly made arrangements for Bill to stay with our good friends, Joyce and Gary; booked the next flight out to Dallas; threw things into a small suitcase; and got a ride to the airport.

My brother-in-law, Joe, picked me up at the airport around 2:00 p.m. Our conversation as we drive to Irving centers on all that has transpired over the past days. Just yesterday I had talked with Mom on the phone. She sounded different; her words were not making sense, and she sounded more confused than ever. She would try to say something but had a hard time speaking, just a groaning clatter. Peggy had told me Mom could not get out of bed, and her pain had increased. Mom had eaten only small portions over the last couple of days. Four days ago Peggy had pushed mom in her wheelchair to the dining hall for her meals, but the next day she refused to leave her room. On Sunday, Mom had read only the front page of the Sunday paper. In the past her habit included reading every page. We learned later that Mom had called and cancelled her subscription to the paper. That Sunday paper would be the last delivery date. I believe Mom knew she would be leaving this world very soon.

I went directly to mom's room. My sister met me at the door, and we hugged. "I'm glad you're here now," Peggy softly cried. Mother looked peaceful as she lay in a coma, even though she labored to breathe. Mom's skin appeared sallow, her checks sunken. I leaned across her chest and whispered in her ears as I cradled her face in my hands, "Mom, this is Barbara. I am here with you now. I love you." I kissed mom's forehead. Her eyes fluttered and opened slightly. "Mom knows I'm here." I tenderly stroked her wrinkled hands. Those are the hands that lovingly cared for me as a baby and young child. The thought of both of my parents no longer here with me seems almost more than I can endure. My dad's passing had been hard, but Mom's would be even harder.

I do not know what to pray for at this moment. I certainly do not want Mom to suffer any longer, but selfishly letting her go is difficult. As I look back on that time in my life, I realize it was OK that I felt I did not know how to pray; the Holy Spirit would pray for me. He would take my "groans" that were too deep for words right to God Himself. And even better than that, the Spirit would know what to pray for in this situation. He would pray according to God's will. Paul said in Romans. 8:26 (NKJV), "Likewise the Spirit also helps in our weaknesses. For we do not know what we should pray for as we ought, but the Spirit Himself makes intercession for us with groaning which cannot be uttered." The times I need God the most, I may not be able to express myself to Him, so His Spirit will do it for me. I just need to allow God's Spirit to take my innermost thoughts, my deepest fears, my longings, to God and let Him pray for me. God gave me peace in those final hours with Mom. He would prepare me to release her into His Hands, and He would give me a deeper reliance on God than I ever had before.

As Mom's body became weaker, something amazing happened. Mom's inner spirit appeared not to be as stressed. She looked calm with a restful peace as God moved her forward into a greater conformity with the character of Christ. Mom's face had a glow; her stress lines appeared to be less. She really looked beautiful. Mother's heart was slowing down, and her breathing was becoming quieter. God's Spirit supported her, renewing Mom in the image of Christ. What I saw in Mom shows me that Paul was right to be so confident that "he who began a good work in you will carry it on to completion until the day of Christ Jesus" (Phil. 1:6).

With Mom's heart barely beating around 8:00 that evening, my sister and I kissed our mother good-bye. We told her it was all right for her to go home to be with the Lord. We wanted so much to keep her with us for as long as possible, but we know that life here on earth meant suffering and pain for her. Mom's face radiated peace as she stopped breathing. The Lord beckoned Mom to her new home. Mother will no longer be in pain and no longer uncomfortable from her broken hip. In my mind I picture my mom and dad together in heaven. I can just hear my dad saying as he waited for mom that night, "What took you so long, Alvenia?" My mother's confidence in what lay ahead for her never wavered. She knew she was heaven bound. My peace and strength in grieving were immeasurably enhanced by the powerful simplicity of mom's faith.

Closing my eyes, I pressed my face into my pillow as tears moistened the pillowcase. My emotions are still fragile over my mom's passing. I will miss her dearly. I find great comfort in Psalm 30:5 (KJV): "Weeping may endure for a night, but joy cometh in the morning." God does not promise exemption from sorrow, but He does promise that while weeping may come for a time it does not have to abide in the dawning of a new day. My intense pain will ease. It will flatten out and not be so encompassing. When I walk through the Valley of Weeping, it will become a place of springs where pools of blessing and refreshment collect after rains! I will be strengthen.

With the rising of the sun, God brings an inward peace. When grief is at its peak, God will bring calmness and a quiet confidence that touches the deepest part of my soul. It is peace with God and peace of God. It is flawless because it is the Lord Himself within me. God whispers into my heart that I had no reason to fear. He Himself had summoned my mother by name, "Welcome home, My child." He had formed and shaped her. He had worked out the details in her life and now in her death. God has transformed my heartache into something good, replacing my weeping with joy.

Journey of Faith 2007

March 1,

It has been several weeks since I had the privilege to give you an update on our journey of faith. God continues to give me many views from this journey. When I walk through valleys, even the valley of death, I do not have to fear. Our great God comforts and leads me. The view from these valleys has given me a new focus on Christ that I wouldn't have gained any other way. Someone once said, "Stars shine brighter in the desert. There are no obstructions, no distractions, no competing lights. The view from the valley isn't so bad because Jesus shines so clearly."

On February 20, I said good-bye to my mother as she left this earth to join her Lord and Savior Jesus Christ. As my sister and I gathered around her bed, we felt the presence of God in that room, and we found comfort and peace. My mom had faith in her Lord. Hebrews 11:1 was a testimony of her life: "Faith is being sure of what we hope for and certain of what we do not see." That day she saw it all, and she is rejoicing and praising the God of heaven and earth who has given her life beyond this earth. I know if my mother could talk to you personally today, she would tell you of the great love of God and how important it is to have a personal relationship with Christ. "It is by grace you have been saved, through faith—and this not from yourselves, it is the gift of God" (Eph. 2:8). "Everyone born of God overcomes the world. This is the victory that has overcome the world, even our faith" (1 John 5:4). "Believe on the Lord Jesus Christ, and you will be saved" (Acts 16:31 NKJV).

When mom's illness ran its course and her body could hold on no longer, she left this world and went to live forever in the presence of God. Mom had God's promise of heaven, and that hope sustained her during her lifetime. That hope is like an anchor for the soul, firm and secure. Mom's earthly body is gone. I'm reminded of the verse, "There is . . . a time to be born and a time to die" (Eccl. 3:1–2). No matter how often we may be miraculously healed or given a new lease on life, someday all of us will look in the mirror and see our bodies are dying. When that time comes, we have God's Word that He has the power to do what he has promised. "My comfort in my suffering is this: Your promise preserves my life" (Ps. 119: 50).

We are blessed when we express to one another and to our gracious heavenly Father the many things for which we are grateful. On my list is thankfulness for my earthly mother, Alvenia Ford. I pay tribute to her and celebrate her life for all that she has meant to our family and to so many friends. She touched my life, and I will forever hold her memory dear to my heart. Those precious memories of life can temper the profound sadness of death. Recalling the cherished details and shared experiences of our lives together. I'm thankful for the memories, the details, fun stories, and the impact of a life.

I will continue to miss my mother, and at times my grief is great. But a gradual lessening of the pain has come as I reflect on all the great promises of God. A special verse is found in Philippians 1:21, "For to me, to live is Christ and to die is gain."

I want to say a special thanks to Gary Alyor, who became Bill's caregiver while I was away. Not only did he oversee Bill's daily medication, his intravenous therapy, but he fed him well. Thanks Nurse Gary. Bill gained four pounds while I was away. I don't know what all you ate, but whatever it was, you did good!

Again, I want to thank all of you from the bottom of my heart for your outpouring of love during my sweet mom's illness and recent home-going. Your compassion and prayers have bought our family immense comfort and strength during this challenging season. During a time with mixed emotions of grief and great joy, Jesus Christ remains the hope of our hearts, and I truly have never loved Him more. How dear you also are to me and how I pray that we will all persevere with ever increasing passion for the precious promises of our eternally faithful God.

With much love and appreciation,
Barbara

Philippians 4:7 "And the peace of God, which surpasses all understanding, will guard your hearts and your minds in Christ Jesus." There is peace in the midst of turmoil. There is joy when eyes are dim. There is perfect understanding when we leave it all to Him.

CHAPTER 23

Reaching the Finish Line
Reflections from the Journey, Days 61–88

What a blessed benefit Jehovah has given to His believing family in giving us access to His throne, but hear Him as He personally invites us to "call to Me, and I will answer you, and show you great and mighty things, which you do not know" (Jer. 33:3 NKJV). The Father of light, in whom there is no variation or shadow of turning, desires to dispense the light of His truth and dispel the darkness of our ignorance. If the great apostle Paul would not have us to be ignorant (see 1 Cor. 10:1), how much more is the plan and purpose of God to reveal spiritual insights enabling us to press on to the finish line that we may grow in the grace and knowledge of our Lord and Savior Jesus Christ.

Journey of Faith 2007

March 7,

God is daily answering your prayers on our behalf. Every day the Lord is renewing Bill's strength, and we see the presence of the Lord in everything that is happening. God has not forsaken us, nor will He ever, and for that we give our heartfelt testimony and our praise to His faithfulness. Today is day 61! Bill is over the hump and sliding down to the finish line. Each day he is feeling stronger and is able to do more than he did the day before. We are walking each day, increasing his stamina and appetite. I now make frequent trips to the grocery store. My goal is to fatten up my husband. Those pounds he lost will come back as he enjoys those nightly chocolate malts made with Blue Bell ice cream.

The doctor continues to reassure us that all is going well, even though there are still some concerns about the ups and downs of Bill's blood work.

In addressing those concerns, Bill has received three Neupogen shots, a growth factor to stimulate the bone marrow to produce extra cells that will move and circulate into the bloodstream. Bill has experienced some body aches due to the bone marrow "working hard." This discomfort is temporary and has already subsided as his cells level out. His white cell count was 14.3 yesterday due to the previous shots. Just think about it: in January his white counts were as low as 0.2. In the next couple of week, we will be able to see exactly what his body will be able to maintain after this boost has run its course. The donor cells, which are Bill's new cells, are like baby cells in his body, and it takes time for them to mature, so the injections give additional growth. I'm reminded that when we become new persons in Christ, our birth is like a baby; we need to grow and mature, which requires taking daily injections of God's Word. "But grow in the grace and knowledge of our Lord and Savior Jesus Christ" (2 Pet. 3:18).

We are doing more of the IV treatments at our apartment, which means we have fewer trips to the clinic. A typical clinic schedule is Monday, Tuesday, and Thursday. The other days the treatment only takes about two and a half hours. This is a real blessing, allowing us more free time.

When Bill was at the clinic yesterday taking his treatment, the doctor came in (typical for Tuesdays) to check on the status of everything. During the course of conversation, Bill asked him about the prospects of going home for Easter and returning on Monday afternoon. After a brief discussion with the lead nurse, the doctor turned to Bill and said, "Since you will be more than ninety days from transplant, I don't have any problem with you going home. In fact, we will go ahead and discharge you, and you can just plan to come back in thirty days." Now to put this in perspective, this does not happen! Patients do not go home prior to one hundred days. God continues "to do exceedingly, abundantly above all that we ask or think" (Eph. 3:20 NKJV). Please pray that Bill remains healthy and is sheltered from any late complications.

By the grace of God we look forward to being at First Baptist Church on Easter Sunday!

Love,
Bill and Barbara

Journey of Faith 2007

March 14,

The boisterous sounds from living in the heart of the city of Houston have etched several impressions upon my mind. Before daybreak the city awakens with streets full of vehicles moving about carrying people to their work destinations. Sounds from the construction sites, beeping noises from the big machinery, metal beams being lifted to high platforms drown out the sweet sounds of birds awakening. The sounds vibrate the ground as new buildings begin to take shape reaching toward the sky. The sounds of our apartment wall clock ticking loudly through the night and the popping sound coming from the refrigerator awakening me from sleep have become part of our city life. But the sounds that have touched me the most are the sounds of people. Help me Lord to come where people are so I can see them and then give me compassion to respond with mercy.

This city of diverse cultures is full of people with many needs. There are the homeless, living under the bridge not far from our apartment, and the poor standing on the corners of city streets desperate for help. Sounds of afflictions and cries for help seem louder living in a city. The sounds of the night sometimes are the most disturbing with sirens from ambulances carrying hurting people to one of the many hospitals within our apartment's radius.

Back home with my comfortable, rather quiet environment sounds, I sometimes do not hear the cries of the people in the small town of Lawrenceburg. Lord, keep my eyes seeing, my ears hearing, and my mind perceiving and don't let me become callous and my heart become dull. But awaken me to hear more clearly those sounds and help me to respond in tender love. What great opportunities I have when I allow God to adjust my hearing to His sounds. May my heart respond and hear sounds of people who have needs. Why is it that God had to send me to a faraway city like Houston in order to readjust my hearing? Maybe I needed this journey more than my husband! Most will agree that we learn more about God during the different and difficult times than when we let self-satisfaction or complacency make us too comfortable.

This journey has been like climbing a mountain. Life is full of mountains we must climb. Sometimes we are so close to the mountain that we lose sight of the mountaintop—God's purposes—because we're struggling with the rocky ledge that's immediately in front of us.

God can always see the top of the mountain even when we are focused on the ledges before us. God's purposes will always represent the very best for our lives and God will bring His purposes to pass. I'm learning to take my hands away from situations and commit them to God, trusting His plans for my life as I climb these mountains. God is bigger than the mountains in my life. He has divine purposes for all situations that I face.

God always has a purpose, but it does not always match our request. We had prayed that God would somehow allow us to stay in this apartment for the remainder of our time in Houston. God had a different plan for us. Our three months limit is coming to an end, and we must move out by the March 19. We have been comfortable in our two-room apartment. The location was perfect for walking back and forth to the hospital. We have our names on several waiting lists for apartments near the clinic. We will know by Thursday regarding a place called "Faith House." A couple we have met referred us to this place, so we will wait to see what God has planned for us. With just a few weeks left, even a motel room would be fine.

Our schedule continues with three days at the clinic, then treatments at the apartment. The donor's blood cells still need assistance with weekly injection of Neupogen. The doctor has discussed taking Bill off all the medicine that prevents graft-versus-host disease, wanting the new cells to become more aggressive in attacking any remaining diseased cells. There appears to be a fine line. A little of the graft-host disease would be good at this point. This would indicate that the new cells are more dominate.

What needs to happen is for the new cells to take complete charge, even if that causes other side effects. As the doctor explained, "We have medicine to control graft host." Pray that those new cells become more aggressive, dominating and attacking the remaining cancer cells.

Yesterday Bill had an ultrasound on his left leg, which has been swelling lately. The doctor wanted to check for any sign of blood clots forming. Results indicated no clots. Every week Bill is putting on a few more pounds. He has even given himself a haircut, well actually just around the ears. His head now has some color. I think it will be curly when it gets longer! We are so thankful for each new sign that Bill's health is improving.

I have started packing a few boxes to send back to Tennessee so our car can carry the remaining load. Bill is excited about the Easter service. He has a sermon ready, and I have already heard parts of it. It has been a long time since he preached, so we might want to bring pillows for our seats that day!

After this week we will not have a Houston address. Please send all correspondence to our Lawrenceburg address. We will certainly miss hearing from you and receiving those cards, but for now we don't have an address for receiving mail.

Looking forward to the celebration of the risen Lord Jesus! He is alive! Heaven's gates are open wide. He is alive! "I am the resurrection and the life. He who believes in Me, though he may die, he shall live" (John 11:25 NKJV).

Love,
Barbara and Bill

Journey of Faith 2007

March 14,

I sent you our weekly newsletter this afternoon, but I can't wait until next week to share this wonderful news of how God works. When we returned from supper this evening, we found a note from Mr. Joe Hightower, the president of Hospitality Apartments, asking us to call him tonight. During the conversation this evening, he asked me if I would be willing to serve as a volunteer assistant manager. With this position comes the privilege of staying in our apartment as long as we need it, while Bill is a patient at M. D. Anderson. Of course I accepted the position and now can share with you our joy and praise to the Lord that we do not have to move. I asked Mr. Hightower what I needed to do for this position, and he said just do what you have already been doing, talking and getting to know the residents. The apartment complex has an office staff that manages the office work, so as a volunteer manager I just need to be available when residents cannot reach the staff.

I'm reminded of what I wrote earlier about God always having a purpose, but it does not necessarily always match our request. Tonight I'm also reminded of another principle relative to God's timing, which is well stated in a quote by Larry Burkett. "God is rarely early, but He is never late." Thank you for your prayers. God continues to provide for us in ways that astound and humble us.

We can continue to receive mail at the Hospitality Apartments until April 6 when we leave to return to Lawrenceburg!

Love,
Barbara & Bill

Journey of Faith 2007

March 26,

Pressing on toward the finish line! That's how I feel as we count down the last days before Bill is discharged and we can journey back to our home in Tennessee. Our wall calendar, visibly seen as you enter our apartment, has each day marked off with a large X. The most beneficial aspect of the calendar is the visual assurance of how Bill has progressed over these months. As I have looked back at the charting of his blood counts, I rejoice, knowing that Bill's physical healing is taking place. New life for Bill is just like last week as we welcomed the first day of spring with all of the trees turning green, roses blooming, and brightly colored flowers displaying the beauty of God's creation. The long winter is gone, and spring brings new life. I feel like we have been restored and renewed. These long months are almost behind us, and in front of us are new beginnings, filling us with an inexpressible and glorious joy.

Now that Bill is on day 80, the doctor has taken Bill off all medicines that prevent graft-versus-host disease (GVH) allowing the new stem cells to be more aggressive. At this point a little GVH would be good, indicating the cells are actively reproducing. We see signs of this as a rash on Bill's face, neck, and upper body. The doctor is not too concerned about this, however, because it is treatable. Not only is the staff watching the skin, but they are keeping a close eye on his organs to ensure they remain healthy. There is a fine line between the new cells recognizing and attacking the diseased cells and keeping them in check so they do not overpower healthy organs or tissue. We want the new cells to see cancer cells as foreign matter and destroy them. But we also want to make sure the donor cells do not attack the healthy parts of the body.

The T cells, the cells that go after any remaining cancer, are now 95 percent donor cells. This is a great improvement as just a month ago they were only 53 percent. The donor T cells become Bill's fighting cells, and they are almost 100 percent! This week Bill will go through some final tests in preparation for next week's discharge.

Today he finished the bone marrow aspiration, a chest X-ray, and a complete PET scan from the skull to mid thigh. On Tuesday and Wednesday he will have blood workups, a CT scan, and two IV therapies.

We no longer have to do treatments at the apartment. The doctor will check Bill tomorrow, and then next Tuesday he will give us the final report from all of the tests. If everything continues to go as well as it is now, we are hoping the last procedure will be the removal of the central venous catheter. I plan to have everything packed; and if possible, we will start the drive on Thursday morning with plans to be back in Lawrenceburg late Friday evening. We can hardly wait!

Every day my heart is full of thanksgiving as I think about each of you who have faithfully prayed for us during this journey. You have been a blessing and encouragement to us, and I know that God has heard the many voices that have been lifted up on our behalf. Bill has come through this treatment, and he is feeling better than he has in months. What a blessing to see God's hand in all of this. When we started this process, Bill had to sign papers that he fully understood all of the risk. There were a great number of anxious moments, but the transplant appears to be successful. To God be the glory!

Over these months we have had opportunity to minister to families who have not experienced success in their loved one's treatments. A patient who lived in the same apartment complex as us died fifteen days after his stem-cell transplant. Last Saturday, Bill and I spent some time with that family helping them with their grief. The wife, Frances, asked Bill to have prayer with her family before they left for Mississippi.

I have been reminded over and over again, as I have walked through this journey, that what I really needed most was to trust in God's promises. He sustained and strengthened me in all circumstances and provided me a residence in His presence no matter what I faced. Our heavenly Father has been in control of our Houston journey and will continue to lead in the days that follow. While most of the time I only saw the step in front of me, God saw the entire journey. He knew what was ahead, and He has been my faithful guide and will be till the end of my days.

Many times I didn't understand what He was doing in my life; comprehending it was hard. But I'm learning to trust Him and believe that His ways for me are good, even when I have had trouble understanding them. What I'm learning about God, both through this journey of faith and through His Word, remind me that I can trust Him both in the difficult times and for our future. God is sovereign, and all things (trials) first pass through His fingers.

I have come to learn that the trials are meant to have application. They provide the classroom for my learning; they are the training ground for my preparedness to serve. I may never fully understand why God allows some inexplicable adversities to enter people's lives, but I can rest in the knowledge that God is faithful and always does right. One day everything will be clearer, resulting in a greater appreciation and love for the God who has redeemed us and called us His own dear children. I can be thankful in all things for my life is a continuous journey of faith. Thank you for allowing me to share some of my life journey experiences through these newsletters.

Bill and I both look forward to our return and reunion with the church family at FBC Lawrenceburg and want to tell each of you who have been our faithful prayer warriors how much we love you and that we will carry a debt of love to you for the rest of our lives.

Love,
Bill and Barbara

CHAPTER 24

There's No Place like Home
Day 88

To my astonishment my packing skills have improved considerably from the start of this journey. I methodically managed to find places in the car for the items we would be carrying back to Tennessee. I must confess, however, that I had already Fed-Exed several boxes, which provided extra space. In my preparation for leaving Houston, I had cleaned out the refrigerator and pantry, giving the remaining food to several apartment residents. Extra medical supplies were dispersed among the patients who had recently arrived at the apartments. We were eager to head to Tennessee, but saying good-bye to the friends we had made over these past months was going to be difficult.

I hugged Boots one last time. In just a few more days she and her husband will also be returning to their hometown of Saint John, Indiana. Boots has given me a loaf of her banana bread along with the recipe to take with us. My emotions teeter between happy to be returning home and yet sad to be leaving the people who have come to mean so much to us during our time in Houston. I will miss their fellowship and the unique bond that has knitted us together because of our similar experiences and challenges. Some of the patients and caregivers have already left to return home, while others are just beginning their journey. Earlier this morning we met Kari and Eric for breakfast to say our good-byes to a couple that will always have a special place in our hearts. Eric is on day 50 of his post stem-cell transplant and is making good progress but still has longer to stay before he can be released.

With the car loaded and having completed most of the preparation for our departure, I decided to take a few more pictures for my memory book. I wanted to capture the apartment complex that has been our home for the past five months. These four building units will eventually be demolished and replaced with new apartments that are being built adjacent to the current buildings. Bill and I have watched some of the early construction work from our apartment's front window.

The expansion project will enable the Hospitality Apartment to reach and touch many more lives through their remarkable ministry. This organization not only provides a place to stay for caregivers and loved ones who are miles away from their homes, but it is a wonderful, caring support system for families facing a lot of tough medical treatments and decisions. Our connection with this ministry has been a great blessing to us, and will continue to be for many more families in the years to come.

Checking to make sure I have not forgotten something, I quickly look through our little two-room apartment one last time. Being assured I have packed all our belongings, Bill takes my hand and leads me to the center of the front room. We kneel beside the couch, and Bill prays, thanking the Lord for all He has done especially for providing this apartment.

I lock the apartment door and take the keys to the management office to say our final good-byes to the volunteer staff. What a blessing to have known these people who have given of their time and support to this ministry. We have met some wonderful people while staying here. We will truly miss them.

Bill wants to drive first, so I lean back in the passenger seat resting my head against the headrest. I observe a look of contentment on Bill's relaxed face as he drives down the highway. I feel so grateful to God for what He has done in my life and in the life of my husband. The God of the universe has heard our prayers, for Bill has survived the rigorous treatments and the early days of this stem-cell transplant. A look at Bill gives evidence of what God has done. He not only is alive, but his health is renewed with more energy than he has felt in months. We were expected to stay longer, but God had other plans.

On day 88, Bill was given permission to return to Nashville. This usually doesn't happen until a patient has completed the full one hundred days or longer. Bill would be released from the hospital's care twelve days earlier. In celebration of the completion of his final treatment, four of the medical staff circled him in the hallway as he was leaving and began singing,

Nah, Nah, Nah, Nah, Nah, Nah, Congratulations you're going home. Hit the road Jack and don't you come back no more, no more, no more!

They also gave him hugs and placed a medallion around his neck depicting a flaming torch. Attached to it was a ribbon with the words, "Who I Am Makes a Difference at M. D. Anderson and I am a Winner!" Later we noticed each of the ATC staff had signed the back of the ribbon with words of encouragement. What a sendoff! Bill would later get another medal in Lawrenceburg when he participated in the Relay for Life walk.

The medical staff told Bill and me there could still be difficult days ahead of us once we returned to Tennessee. Dealing with possible side effects and the long-term physical complications some survivors can face concerns me. We were told to watch for any signs or symptoms of infection, especially the possibility of issues with GVHD. Finding problems early and treating them aggressively would be important. I am glad Bill's Houston doctors have arranged for a doctor at Nashville's Vanderbilt University Medical Center to oversee any immediate needs Bill might have once we get back home. However, Bill will still travel back to M. D. Anderson for follow-up visits during the first year after transplant. Before leaving the hospital, Bill was given a detailed instruction sheet of what he can and cannot do while taking the required transplant medications.

Driving past the state line of Texas into Louisiana, I watched the transformation of the scenery from the big cities to the open fields. While watching the changes in scenery all around me, I reflected on the many life adjustments we had made over these past months. I know our future will hold some additional scenery alteration as we transition back home. Caring for Bill and picking up our lives back in Tennessee could be demanding.

Returning to my job means I will not be as involved with Bill's daily care. That concerns me greatly. Bill will need to be extremely careful not to be exposed to other people's germs or to be around sick people. His occupation involves contact with people so he will have to take certain precautions, especially avoiding large crowds. He will need to limit his time in the sun, wear sunscreen and long-sleeved shirts, and avoid yard work and dusty places. Bill was told to be extremely careful around young children, especially new babies who have just had their shots. That would be hard since our daughter will be giving birth to a grandson in June.

For several more months Bill will have to continue to avoid fresh fruits and vegetables while also maintaining his weight by eating high-calorie foods and plenty of protein. The doctor told Bill he could resume most of his normal activities in moderation but would need to increase his daily activities slowly due to tiring easily. Knowing my husband, he might not pace himself. He will want to return to his busy schedule as quickly as possible in spite of still dealing with fatigue and other changes his body might demand.

The closer we get to Tennessee the faster Bill drives. I shift back and forth in my seat watching the miles pass, and I get more excited as we near home. Bill felt like driving so he actually is at the wheel for most of the trip. What a difference from the time we made the initial drive in December. Bill had been so sick he slept most of the journey.

We stopped in Mississippi that night but woke up eagerly ready to travel the last leg of the drive. People from our church keep calling to find out our location. Several people were apparently keeping track of our itinerary. When Bill went to pick up our mail the day after we arrived home, the postman said, "I understand you spent the night before last in Mississippi." We had a good laugh about living in a small town where everyone seems to know the whereabouts of everyone.

As we turn onto the main road leading to our familiar subdivision, I say to Bill, "Look at all the yellow ribbons. This must be for a local soldier who has returned from the war." However, as we round the corner, I realize the yellow ribbons are for us. I could not believe what I see! What an unbelievable sight as we drive down our street seeing mailboxes decorated and ribbons placed on sticks lining the roadway. A cluster of people wait on our front yard. My heart leaps as I see our home and the huge sign welcoming us home. We are absolutely overwhelmed by what we see.

Several of our church members, friends, and neighbors took on the project of cleaning our house, landscaping our yard, and restocking the pantry and refrigerator with food. What they did for us is just incredible. Bill and I are deeply moved by the sweet spirit of generosity shown to us. They are the most awesome people anywhere! Bill and I have felt so blessed by the outpouring of love and the many acts of kindness shown to us while we were away and especially now as we return home. There really is no place like home!

I cannot think of a better place to be than right here. Bill and I have been so touched by all the expressions of love. We received so many cards while we were away that I had filled two boxes. I plan to keep every card. God touched us through so many Godly people. Allowing people to care for you can be hard. Sometimes it is easier for people to be givers instead of receivers, but cancer can put you in the latter category more than you probably like. I am forever grateful that God taught me some lessons about receiving as well as how blessed it is to give.

Shortly after returning home, our children and grandchildren arrived for a wonderful and emotional reunion. The two grandchildren swarmed Bill like bees on a honeysuckle vine. They clung to his legs and squealed with excitement. Bill and I must have hugged and kissed them all a dozen times as we wrapped them in our arms! It was so good to see them and especially to be with family here in our Tennessee home. The word *home* reverberated right through my heart, as little Kayelynn said, "Papa, I'm so glad you're home." A huge lump filled my heart as I thought about the meaning behind the simple greeting.

Following supper Bill is seated on the couch with our granddaughter, who was not going to leave his side. She was determined Bill would not leave again so she hung on to him tightly; however, later during the evening, she leaves the room and returns with something hidden behind her back. Her mother is beside her as she begins to tell Bill that Kayelynn has something for him. She explains, "Kayelynn had her hair cut several months ago, and because she was so concerned about her grandpa's bald head, she asked me if she could save a lock of her hair to give to you when you return home." Kayelynn with a wide grin on her face brings her little hands around clasping something in one. She slowly opens her hand revealing the golden locks of hair tied together with a string. No gift could have touched Bill more deeply than the precious hair from his granddaughter as she gave it to her Papa. Bill's tear-filled eyes received it gladly. That lock of hair is placed on a bookshelf in Bill's study beside Kayelynn's picture. It will remain there permanently.

I learned some things about helping little children understand what is going on when a family member has cancer. One thing to do is take time to comfort a child who may be distraught about a loved one's cancer. Our family decided to be open with our grandchildren about what their papa was going through. We felt honest and open communication would help them deal with Bill's cancer and would lovingly include them in what was going on in our lives while we were in Houston. Our daughter talked to Will and Kayelynn about their Papa's illness. I will never forget the first time the grandchildren saw their Papa without any hair. "I liked it better when you had hair," Will spoke directly to his grandfather. Bill laughed and said, "I liked it better too when I had hair." Bill gave the grandchildren time to ask questions and share their feelings. I learned never to underestimate even the youngest child's ability to feel the stress and fear associated with battling cancer.

I also learned how important it is to communicate regularly with grandchildren while you are away from them. The time we were in Houston we stayed in contact with the children by talking over the phone as well as sending notes and cards. It was important to tell them how much we loved them and to reassure them we were doing well. Our grandchildren sent us pictures they had drawn, and their mother kept us connected with photographs she had taken of them. We covered our apartment walls with those beautiful images.

Kayelynn had a kindergarten project in which she had made a two-foot long cutout portrait of herself. She sent "Flat Kayelynn" to us explaining that we were to take Flat Kayelynn along with us wherever we went. We were to take pictures and then write a story about her adventures. You can image Flat Kayelynn had many interesting escapades while we were in Texas. In one depiction Flat Kayelynn was propped up next to Bill in his hospital room while Bill's doctor joined in on the fun.

That first Sunday back we had a great homecoming celebration with our church family. It was a glorious service. The church had prayed Bill would be able to return home in time to preach the Easter service. God was answering those prayers far beyond our wildest expectations as Bill and I walked into the worship center that morning.

My first indication that God was doing something special was the crowd. The room was packed with people, one large mass of members and guests. They stood and clapped as we entered. It was not until Bill came to the podium to welcome everyone that he saw his brothers, Bob and Bruce. What a wonderful surprise and blessing! Bill's prayer was full of emotion as he prayed, thanking God for His grace and goodness. Tears filled my eyes as I saw what God was doing throughout the morning as Bill preached the sermon God had laid on his heart. Many others said later they too had tears coming down their faces from the beginning of the service right until the final amen, praising God for His faithfulness. I was overwhelmed with thanksgiving and praise to God.

No church anywhere had been more supportive and benevolent in caring for their pastor than this church. Our church family hung in there with us from the beginning and demonstrated their determination to walk with us to the conclusion of this journey. How assuring to know we have the presence of a gracious and powerful God and a church family that fervently prayed for us daily. "The effective, fervent prayer of a righteous man (congregation) avails much," says James 5:16 (NKJV). The church family's prayers on our behalf visited heaven with frequency and earnestness over the past many months while we were in Houston. I could almost hear the brush of angels' wings as those heavenly beings sent forth to minister to those who will inherit salvation busied themselves with our every hurt and anxiety. I am sure that Bill and I personally worked a few of them overtime!

I marveled at the way God took care of the smallest of details in everyday matters and learned firsthand that "God is rarely early, but He is never late." Times are in His hands, and in His wisdom and purpose He manifests His will for us. I cannot recall a moment when divine providence did not anticipate and provide for our every need. Often many of our friends were the caring agents through which we received our "daily bread" or found that extra strength from their numerous cards and phone calls. I wish Bill and I could show everyone in some tangible way just how precious each of them was to us, but lacking proper and adequate means, please know that we love you, every one, and thank our God upon every thought and memory of you. We, like the apostle Paul, "give thanks to God always for you all, making mention of you in our prayers, remembering without ceasing your work of faith, labor of love, and patience of hope in our Lord Jesus Christ" (1 Thess. 1:2–3 NKJV).

Bill and I are so happy to be back in Tennessee, April 2007! There really is no place like home. We are ready to renew our energies and focus on all that our Lord would have us do by exalting Christ and loving people.

CHAPTER 25

Houston, We Have Remission

The success of NASA space mission is not determined by its going into space but by the safe return of its astronauts. When we left Houston on April 4, 2007, Bill and I did not know the full success of the transplant. A month later when we returned for our first follow-up visit, we would hear these words, "Bill you are in remission." The return of the spaceship to the Houston Space Center brings a time of great jubilation, celebration, and thanksgiving; likewise, I was experiencing similar emotions on our return trip to Houston. After seeing Bill battling a dreaded disease for eight years, he would finally be in remission. God was good, for He had allowed Bill to overcome overwhelming odds. His stem-cell transplant had been a success. I give thanks and praise to the Father for His goodness and protection. It's a beautiful thing to give thanks to God. I will praise the Lord!

Bill had been released before the one hundred days, which usually doesn't happen. I felt God had orchestrated the early date so Bill could preach at our home church on Easter Sunday. When Bill's doctor entered the examination room, I knew the news would be good. He had the biggest grin on his face when he said: "The test results are back, and it is looking good! The bone marrow aspiration and blood report are showing the donor stem cells are not only reproducing, but they are maturing." He went on to say, "The CT scan and chest x-ray show no signs of cancer." From a medical standpoint this is a victory for Bill, for the treatment protocol, and for future patients.

Even greater is the wonderful testimony of how God's grace had sustained and allowed me to see His purposes in putting this cancer in remission. To God be the glory for the great thing He has done. I felt humbled to be receiving this good news. I knew without a doubt God had blessed us beyond measure with this gift of remission. As Bill reached out to shake his doctor's hand, he said, "I want to thank God and thank you for the success of the transplant." Bill's doctor replied. "Don't thank me. Just thank God."

Scripture clearly teaches that God uses others to accomplish His purposes. I felt the partnership of so many who prayed and advocated heaven's throne of grace on our behalf. God had used these prayer warriors along with the skilled staff at M. D. Anderson to accomplish what He was doing in Bill's life.

Psalm 54:4 (NKJV) says, "Behold, God is my helper; the Lord is with those who uphold my life." In the margin of Bill's Bible, he had written by this verse the words, "my doctors." We have faithfully prayed for the doctors and nurses who have attended to Bill's needs during the transplant process. They were wonderful. We could not have asked for a more skilled, professional, and compassionate staff at MDA. God was with those who upheld Bill's life. We are thankful for each one's part in restoring Bill's health.

I have often thought that the medical staff cared for Bill like earthly angels. I think about how angels are often romanticized or portrayed in humorous ways in movies and books. That's the way, Clarence, in the classic holiday movie *It's a Wonderful Life*, was portrayed. Yet angels aren't people who have died and then changed into their heavenly form. According to the Bible, angles are an entirely different created order of celestial beings whose primary purpose is to praise God and communicate God's messages to the rest of us. Doctors and nurses aren't literal angels, but I think they are as close as most of us will ever see. I always want to find ways to show my appreciation to the hospital staff and other special people God uses to accomplish His purposes.

The first month after returning home from the initial transplant, I saw Bill's health being restored. His energy level and appetite continued to increase. Bill embraced life with a new vigor and excitement. He wanted to get up and go! The wonderful changes in Bill's overall health gave several indications that his disease was under control. Even his hair took on a new look. It came back curly and with the texture of a baby's hair. I love running my hand through those gorgeous, curly locks. Now Bill's doctor has confirmed what I already knew in my heart: God has done a miracle!

All the visible signs and symptoms of cancer have disappeared. Although cancer could still be in Bill's body, undetected, I have an incredible peace that is hard for me to describe. I am experiencing a victory, and I want to shout it from the highest mountaintop. I feel like Bill and I have done our part to combat this cancer, but I will not judge whether we have beaten it by whether Bill is in remission or cured. We will beat it no matter what because Bill and I have refused to let it prevail over us and control our lives. This good news enhances my feelings of triumph, for I have learned to find the victory moment by moment. God's peace will direct my thoughts, not the cancer. I defeat cancer hour by hour as I remember that God's power within me is greater than the cancer. I overcome cancer day by day when I put my trust in God's strength and not in cancer's weakness. Anyone can beat cancer because being victorious is not about being in remission or cured. It is about a relationship with the Lord Jesus Christ who gives us victory in all things.

I learned early in this cancer journey that once you have cancer, it can continue to raise its ugly head in your life for a long time. Bill could relapse. There is no guarantee cancer will remain in remission. Bill will need to be monitored for cancer for the rest of his life. Because of the stem-cell transplant, Bill's disease is now in remission; but I know he will have to undergo maintenance treatment for years to come. Whipping cancer is not a one-moment or a one-day or a once-for-all accomplishment. God has given me a clearer understanding about beating cancer, and one thing I know for sure is I have determined to live victorious in the power of Jesus Christ. I will put my trust in Jesus. He is the only guarantee I have; that is what makes life with cancer possible.

The Houston stem-cell transplant, like a NASA space mission, has been successful. Bill has survived, and the astronauts have returned safely to earth. With both feet on this planet, Bill's health is energized with a fresh determination to live each day to the fullest rather than putting off the important things for the future. One good thing cancer did was to help me focus on the important things in life. I think survivors have a greater appreciation of life and perhaps have new priorities. I know that is true for the Betts family.

Not only did Bill and I receive the wonderful news about his remission on that first follow-up return trip to Houston in May, but we shared in another celebration. Bill had the opportunity to perform the marriage ceremony for Eric and Kari. Both of them had decided they did not want to postpone their wedding date any longer. Even though Eric had not been released from the hospital, they both wanted to go forward with the marriage union. They were so connected in their love for each other. Kari had not let Eric's cancer change her commitment and devotion to the man God had brought into her life.

Kari had met Eric the summer of 2005. She had worked as a physician assistant (PA) in the same doctor's office where Eric practiced. One year later Eric was diagnosed with leukemia. They had talked with Bill about conducting the wedding service once Eric was released and they could return to Albuquerque. Now they had decided not to wait any longer. When they learned that Bill and I would be back in Houston the first week of May, Kari quickly planned a beautiful wedding for Friday evening, May 4, 2007.

It was one of the sweetest ceremonies I have ever attended. It was also a first for M. D. Anderson with both the groom and the minister being stem-cell transplant patients. The wedding took place in the hospital chapel. Many of Eric's and Kari's family and friends flew to Houston for the special occasion. Some of the doctors and nurses from the hospital were also there to celebrate with Eric and Kari. Kari was a radiant bride as she stood next to Eric committing her love and devotion to him.

In the months following the wedding, Bill traveled back to Houston for four follow-up visits. Each time Bill was able to visit with this special couple. Bill and I love them like our own children. Eric did not get to go home after the one hundred days because of numerous complications. In April, Eric lost sight in his right eye. The blindness in that eye never got him down, for he always looked at life positively focusing on the future. The strong bond of friendship continued to evolve during that year as we kept in contact. Bill did not mind all of those follow-up visits to Houston, knowing that he would get to see Eric and Kari.

For the remainder of 2007, Bill received great reports from his Houston doctor. He heard those wonderful words, "Bill you are still in remission with no signs of CLL." The cancer cells were no longer sapping the life out of Bill, and no signs of cancer could be detected in his body. Bill knew he needed to continue with those post-transplant precautions even though eventually all of his medications were eliminated. During each visit we were told to watch for any side effects that might come within that first year post transplant. Some side effects could even be long-term producing late complications. Regaining normal blood counts could take awhile to happen so we anticipated Bill might need platelet transfusions at some point, which he did.

Bill did come down with a bad case of shingles the early part of the summer. This is a viral infection that usually produces a painful skin rash that follows the underlying route of nerves inflamed by the virus. This is the same virus that causes chicken pox. Twenty to 50 percent of patients develop the shingles infection during the first year post-transplant, usually after the third month.

Bill also developed a secondary cancer about four months after we got back. He had a squamous cell carcinoma on his forehead, which he promptly had removed by a local dermatologic surgeon. The surgeon used the "Moe's" method, which is a micrographic controlled surgery designed to spare as much normal skin as possible.

We had been told stem-cell survivors could experience some cognitive problems dealing with how the brain processes information such as memory lapses, poor concentration, stuttering, difficulty spelling, inability to perform jobs previously mastered, and difficulty learning new tasks. However, most survivors find ways to adapt to these changes like making lists or leaving notes around the house to remind them of things they need to do. Most of these side effects can be resolved over time. Bill only experienced slight cognitive deficits such as sporadic memory lapses. He had to work hard on concentrating especially during his preparation for his sermons. But for the most part he handled these little issues well.

Bill and I wanted to use this transplant experience to benefit others so every opportunity that came our way we were ready to share or do whatever we could to help others who were also going through similar difficulties. In August 2007 Bill and I participated in the local Relay for Life. Bill encouraged other cancer patients to remain optimistic about their condition and never to give up. He was able to give a brief account of our journey with cancer. Through it all he pointed everyone present to a loving, powerful God who works in building up the spiritual side of each of us as well as the physical. Success stories are not just about survivors but also those who come to know God in a more intimate way.

Thanks to early detection and much improved treatments, millions of Americans are surviving cancer. There are more than ten million survivors in the United States and more than 22.4 million worldwide. Today many types of cancers are either curable or chronic, which means that patients can live through the cancer or with the cancer for many years.

Patients and caregivers need to ask their doctors if there are clinical trials out there for their specific disease that could potentially benefit them. Bill and I chose not to believe a doctor's diagnose, and Bill is alive today. There are clinical trials for patients with every conceivable disease stage and situation. The treatment plans today are because someone went on a clinical trial, thus paving the way for many patients to benefit because of the information gained from those trials. A key element in getting good care is knowledge about your treatment choices.

My desire is to be an advocate for cancer patients who choose to have stem-cell transplants. Many clinical studies involving stem-cell research are currently helping patients find a new hope for cure. But many patients' anticipation is dashed when they find out a lot of clinical trials aren't covered by insurance. Often patients do not have the extra money to cover the cost so their hopes are shattered when their insurance company denies coverage for the routine cost associated with clinical trial participation, deeming it experimental treatment. Nearly half of our country has state laws requiring insurance carriers to cover routine care to patients in clinical trials. Medicare patients have been covered since 2001. However, some states do not have this. This becomes a problem for patients when they consider leaving their family with large debt. So most of the time, patients choose not to go the route of a clinical trial that could possibly save their lives.

Many survivors have difficulty obtaining health and individual life insurance policies after their transplant. Bill had health insurance; however, his premiums tripled in cost one year after transplant. Often families are left with high health care bills due to inadequate insurance coverage. My desire is to support patients and caregivers who face obstacles that appear to have no way around them.

Patients and caregivers will face many challenges as they battle with the struggles that come with having a disease. I know because Bill and I have encountered hurdles, but they are hurdles that can be overcome with God's help. Time and again God continues to help us over the obstacles that awaited us, which in turn help us reach out to others who are facing similar situations. God helps us remain calm and confident that we will complete the race He has called us to run. Our God is a big God, and He can make low any high hurdle before us. The words "Houston We Have Remission" give evidence of one hurdle we went over.

On a wall in one of the hospital hallways of the bone marrow transplant floor is a display called the "BMT Wall of Survivors." Pictures and stories of transplant survivors are exhibited. I recalled reading those stories while Bill was hospitalized. It had brought great encouragement to me as I read about the lives of patients who had survived their transplant and were living a healthier life. They had been through extraordinary experiences and were testimonies that cancer can be defeated. I remember thinking back then, *One day my husband's story and picture will be on that wall.* I just recently had a new photo made of Bill. It is ready to go on the "BMT Wall of Survivors."

I will praise God for His love. "And I know and believed the love that God has for me" (see 1 John 4:16). I will praise Him for His grace. "Where sin abounded, grace abounded much more" (Rom. 5:20 NKJV). I will praise Him for His Son. "For God so loved the world that he gave his one and only Son" (John 3:16). I will praise Him for His spiritual blessings. "Who has blessed me with every spiritual blessing in the heavenly places in Christ Jesus" (see Eph. 1:3). Having experienced His grace and mercy, I know God is good. God is good all the time. I know without a doubt that God had blessed me immeasurably.

CHAPTER 26

Relapses Can Happen

I could not understand why the doctors were so insistent that Bill return to M. D. Anderson so soon. He had just completed his first year checkup in January 2008, and Bill's bone marrow aspiration test results had indicated the donor cells were at 100 percent. Bill looked good and felt wonderful with the exception of occasional fatigue, which I attributed to his busy schedule. The only small indication there might be a problem was a few of his lymph nodes showed a slight increase in size. I was hoping the enlargement of the nodes was due to a lingering cold. Bill's doctor didn't see it that way because he wanted to do another CT and CAT scan in March. We tried to get the tests scheduled locally so Bill would not have to make the trip to Houston, but for reasons we would learn later, God wanted Bill in Houston.

On Monday, March 3, Bill flew to Houston anticipating staying only a couple of days. Bill's plan was to see his doctor on Thursday morning after his tests were completed, and then he was to fly back to Nashville in the afternoon. Schedules got changed. Bill did not fly back to Nashville, but instead I flew to Houston. Bill's platelets had dropped down in single digits, which necessitated a platelet transfusion and required him to be admitted to the ACT treatment center. He also received another intravenous treatment to boost his blood counts, which resulted in a negative reaction, giving me great concerns about what was happening.

Bill's CT scan showed lymph nodes in the abdomen/pelvis enlarging along with several in his neck area. A small shadow in his lungs also indicated a problem. Since the size of the lymph nodes had escalated from the January scans and the bone marrow indicated an increase of atypical lymphoid cells, the doctor felt this was consistent with recurrent of CLL/small lymphocytic lymphoma. Because the pathology reports from the bone marrow findings were suggestive but not conclusive, the doctor had requested a fine needle aspiration to confirm recurrence.

The fine needle aspiration took place on Monday, followed by a meeting with Bill's doctor. Our suspicions were confirmed. Bill had relapsed 430 days after his allogeneic transplant. The doctor told Bill: "The fine needle aspiration reveals small lymphocytic lymphoma/CLL. Your disease has come back." Bill and I were finding ourselves returning to a previous episode in our lives that we thought was behind us. Relapses can be hard on both the patient and caregiver especially as I thought about what lay in front of us. At the moment, however, I was feeling a bit like what Paul expressed in 2 Corinthians 4:8, "perplexed, but not in despair." "If God is for us, who can be against us?" (Rom. 8:31). Now as then, I knew Bill and I would find the grace and strength of our sovereign God more than sufficient as we faced these new events, opportunities and challenges.

Bill's doctor explained to us that some patients who relapse after transplant can be put back in remission by infusing them with more of the donor's cells. He discussed at length the possible treatment options for recurrent disease. Two possibilities seemed to be good options.

The first protocol would require a donor lymphocyte infusion (DLI) with four series of Rituxan. The lymphocytes are a type of white blood cell. These cells have a number of roles in the immune system, including the production of antibodies and other substances that fight infection and cancer. Bill needed to have a boost to enhance the function of his immune system and to attack the recurrent disease.

The other alternative would be the use of NK cells and Rituxan. Both of these protocols would require Bill to stay in Houston for at least six weeks to receive the treatments. If Bill could not stay in Houston, he might possibly have the Rituxan done in Nashville and then come back to Houston for the DLI.

We made the decision to follow the protocol for the DLI. Bill's brother would return to Houston to give more stem cells. A Nashville doctor at Vanderbilt University Medical Center kindly agreed to give Bill the Rituxan treatments during the next four weeks. Bill would then return to M. D. Anderson for the DLI. The stem cells would be infused between the second and third dose of Rituxan.

We had been informed at the beginning of our transplant journey that even though transplants could be successful, they were not always a cure. Recurrence can occur after the transplant. Bill's doctors had explained that some patients who relapse after transplant can be put back into remission by infusing them with more of the donor's cells. Bill would need a boost, sort of like a jump-start. These donor cells would help destroy the diseased cells still lingering in Bill's body. Bill was ready to go forward with the plan.

The doctor explained that the procedure was like having a mini-transplant. Bill's brother, Bruce, would donate additional stem cells, and then a small portion of the recollected lymphocytes would be infused into Bill.

We were told that the side effects from this type of infusion are less than those experienced by standard stem-cell transplant; however, there could still be a risk of developing graft-versus-host disease or other complications. The possible benefits would be to improve disease control and prolongation of survival. Bill signed another consent paper authorizing the procedure.

On March 25, Bill received the DLI as an outpatient without any complications. The completed procedure took about three hours including the premedication of Benadryl and Tylenol. A thorough crosscheck of the stem-cell bag identification was confirmed with product number and donor name. The infusion was administered through a peripheral IV in his arm. A nurse remained in the Apheresis Center to ensure Bill tolerated the cells and to perform frequent vital sign checks.

The only side effect Bill had during the infusion was a slight flushing of the face. Because the cells had been frozen, Bill experienced a strong, metallic taste in his mouth during the infusion. This taste was from a preservative that aids in preserving the cells. Bill sucked on pieces of hard candy during the infusion to lessen the taste. For several hours after the infusion, an unusual odor described as garlic, tomato juice, and creamed corn could be detected. I think I prefer Bill's normal aftershave over this scent.

With the relapse of Bill's cancer came the decision to alter his schedule. On the advice of doctors and close friends, Bill set aside his responsibilities as full-time pastor. Bill needed ample time to rest and get the cancer back into remission. I didn't want all of this to be happening, and I wasn't sure what other complications lie ahead for us; but in spite of my feelings, I knew I did not need to trust in appearances or even those unsettling thoughts. I was to look at the promises found in God's Scriptures. *The Message* paraphrases 2 Corinthians 4:8–9 this way: "We've been surrounded and battered by troubles, but we're not demoralized; we're not sure what to do, but we know that God knows what to do; we've been spiritually terrorized, but God hasn't left our side; we've been thrown down, but we haven't broken." My faith in the will of God carries me through this time regardless of what the outcome will be. It will take me into any uncharted waters, making it possible for me to walk above the turbulence and waves. I cannot imagine how those who have no faith go through times like these. Without God there is no hope.

I may not have the final outcome of this recent mini-transplant, but I do know the final, permanent, eternal, forever outcome for all those who belong to God. I know beyond a shadow of a doubt God loves me even though He is allowing all of these things to happen to Bill. This life is not all there is. If Bill is to die from cancer, I know where Bill will spend eternity because of his personal relationship with God through His Son, Jesus. Life may not seem fair to have to experience all these setbacks, but God has provided salvation, and heaven is a reality for Bill and me. The Scriptures say there will be no more pits, no more tears, no more sickness, no more relapses, and no more dying. Now that makes sense to me. That is my ultimate hope.

If you are a believer in Jesus, you cannot lose your battle with cancer or any other disease. When a believer dies, it may appear temporarily that death has won, but appearances can be deceiving. During those times we need to focus on God's eternal perspective and not on cancer or earthly death. I know how hard it is to have this eternal perspective, for we have a tendency to cling to life here because it's all we know and see. But whether I live ten years or a hundred, it's a blink of the eye compared to the eternity I'll spend in heaven.

I derive great consolation and strength from God's Word, knowing that death is swallowed up in victory. Jesus tasted death so that we could taste of His goodness. Our good friend Dr. Eric Thomas is in the presence of Christ experiencing no more suffering and pain from his short battle with leukemia. Eric's earthly death took place on March 22, 2008. Eric was thirty-seven years old. Remember, I told you I did not understand why Bill had to keep returning back to Houston. One of the reasons, I believe, was that God wanted us to be near Kari and Eric during those last months of Eric's life and especially while he remained in the intensive care unit. (ICU)

Eric never was released from the care of M. D. Anderson, even though in October 2007, his body did show signs of being cancer free. Bill and I still smile when we recall the question Eric asked his doctor when he was finally told he was in remission. "Does this mean I can buy a big tube of toothpaste?"

Eric had such a desire to live even though he experienced so many setbacks. He became a wheelchair-bound patient; however, seldom have I seen a man with such a strong tenacity, for he seemed never to give up, always holding on, always pressing on, and always expecting the impossible to happen. Eric had such an optimistic and fun-loving spirit, and he felt he could beat his disease. He was determined to overcome any obstacles. Eric told us, "I'm too stubborn to quit and too stupid to know better." But fighting the setbacks and the many rigorous treatments became difficult, and finally his body could not endure.

Why did Eric not experience a miraculous healing when others do? I do not have answers to many unresolved and lingering questions as to why some people get cured of cancer and some don't. Sometimes death will never make sense for a family that loses a love one. The pain never goes away. There are no easy answers to what appears to be the unfairness of life. Just because a person has faith in God does not always mean God will keep hard times, trials, sufferings away, and even death away; but I do know what God can do as a result of going through those difficult times.

Physical healings are absolutely wonderful, but they may not be the ultimate way God heals. He has the power to heal more than just the cancer, for the Bible tells us God is Jehovah Raphe, the One who heals. Don't ever doubt that God can heal, but don't ever limit Him to just one way to heal. When death came to Eric, the only conclusion I have is that in the providence of God it was Eric's time to go. In the midst of it all, I believe there is hope and peace in the certainty that heaven's glory awaits those who have put their trust and faith in Jesus Christ alone for their salvation. I believe that is God's ultimate healing and that is how people make it through something like the death of a love one. Facing death is really the ultimate triumph for a Christian.

Eric now knows the answers to those hard questions. He is in perfect peace. The moment Eric died, the pearly gates of heaven flew open, and in walked Eric Thomas with a new body, a body that was no longer held captive by leukemia; and there to greet him was Christ, ready to start Eric's next journey.

Kari asked Bill to do the memorial service for Dr. Eric Anthony Thomas, her beloved husband of only eleven short months. The memorial service for Eric took place Saturday, April 5, at Sagebrush Community Church, in Albuquerque, New Mexico. Bill and I arrived late Friday evening after Bill has completed his last Rituxan treatment at Vanderbilt Medical Center in Nashville.

The service was a great tribute to Eric's life. Several people spoke about his athletic accomplishments and his professional achievements. However, Bill told the crowd of about three hundred that he did not know Eric when he played basketball for the University of New Mexico; nor did he know Eric as a spinal surgeon. Bill knew Eric as a fellow patient dealing with a disease that was bigger than each of them. Bill shared with everyone that what made Dr. Thomas one of his heroes was Eric's relationship with Jesus Christ. That relationship happened while Eric was at M. D. Anderson.

Over the months of Bill's acquaintance with Eric, Bill saw a growing and deepening faith in Eric's heart. A faith that said Jesus Christ was his Savior and Lord. A faith that revealed itself in a peace that Eric would be alright no matter what happened with his life. "Therefore, having been justified by faith, we have peace with God through our Lord Jesus Christ."(Rom. 5:1 NAS) His faith gave evidence that he was now ready for the inevitable. Eric's countenance and the words that he spoke gave evidence of a deep, abiding faith. "You will keep him in perfect peace, whose mind is stayed on You" (Isa. 26:3 NKJV). Even during the last hours of Eric's life, with the annoyance of tubes and machines, Eric found comfort in knowing that leaving this world was not the end for him but the beginning of a much better life.

Jesus Christ was the big difference Bill saw in Eric's life that enabled Eric to face the new trials each day, and he did so with such grace and strength. During the conclusion of the service, Bill shared the gospel and gave an invitation for those present who would like to invite Christ into their hearts and trust Him as their Savior and Lord. Only God knows the response that day, but we are OK with leaving the results with Him.

Eric's brother, Brent, shared these thoughts about Eric at the memorial service:

> As I spent time reflecting on Eric's life, I started to think about who my brother was and what people might not know about him. It is easy to talk about his athletic accomplishments or the fact that he became a surgeon, but I do not think that is what Eric would want me to talk about today. As I reflected back at his life and specifically the last 18 months, I can honestly say that his diagnosis led to the most significant event and journey that would lead to one life-changing friendship and an eternity-changing relationship. This journey included two men who did not know each other. One lived in Albuquerque and the other lived in Tennessee. They were on different paths that might not have ever crossed if it weren't for a greater plan. Both of these men were diagnosed with different diseases at different times, but they met each other in Houston while both were recovering from stem-cells transplants. This meeting would change the course of Eric's life not only here on Earth but for eternity. This man would not only marry Eric and Kari, and speak at his memorial service, but more importantly, this man connected with Eric as no other single person ever had. I believe that Eric saw Christ in him. Although Eric knew there was a God before meeting Bill, Bill's example of Christ's love led to Eric's eventual acceptance of Christ in his heart.
>
> I honestly never thought I would see such a dramatic change in my brother. But over the last year, I saw Eric's earthly confidence, intellect, and drive transform into a person who truly understood the meaning and purpose of life. I saw more love and gentleness from him as he battled his disease every day. I was always astonished by the grace he showed to everybody, even during the darkest of days. This grace and peace can only be explained by a life that was transformed by the love of Christ.

As a brother it was hard to watch Eric suffer and go through so much this last year, but the time he spent here with us is just a vapor compared to the time he will spend in eternity. Although, it is hard to understand why somebody has to be taken so young, I see how Eric's radical transformation will glorify Christ and affect so many lives for years to come.

It is hard to understand why certain things occur in life, Eric dying at the height of his career, the loss of both my parents, and Bill's brother Dave dying in 2009, one week after he learned that he had a rare, aggressive type of non-Hodgkin lymphoma know as Burkitt. He had been in remission all these years and had remained healthy until that last month. Those happenings and other events are hard to comprehend.

In the summer of 2008, Bill and I moved closer to Nashville where Bill is being cared for by a wonderful team of doctors at Vanderbilt University Medical Center. The staff at the Vanderbilt Stem Cell Transplant Medical Group is giving Bill the best treatment options available. We are so grateful for the hematology clinic and all that they are doing with stem cell research. Bill has received two additional donor lymphocyte infusion (DLI) while at Vanderbilt. He also participated in an experimental drug; but was taken out of the program after several rounds of treatment because it was not producing the desired results. Through all of these procedures Bill remains in good shape able to continue most of his routines. We enjoy life and actually do what most healthy people can do. Just looking at my husband you would never know that he has cancer.

In January of 2009, Bill had surgery to remove a small tumor on his right arm that had been identified as melanoma. That procedure also involved removing tissue around the tumor and several lymph nodes which did come back as normal; however, later in October, the skin cancer did return and invaded some lymph nodes. Bill had twenty-five lymph nodes removed under his right arm; however, only three were infected with melanoma. These two types of cancers are presenting some major challenges for his doctors. In spite of these setbacks, God shows His faithfulness, mercy, and love as Bill continues his ongoing battle with these ugly faces of cancer that just want go away.

Bill wrote this email to some friends.

We serve a sovereign God who is more than able to do exceedingly, abundantly above all that we can ask or even think. I never doubt His ability to change and heal any and every aspect of my body; the exciting part is to see how He gives me so much

strength when I'm so weak. When I first was diagnosed with cancer, I yielded my life, body, and ministry to the Lord to do not only what was best but also what was His perfect will for my life. Healing was the one thing I left totally to His discretion for knowing that we have this Treasure in an earthen vessel my interest was more that the Treasure be seen than that the vessel be noticed. His strength is always perfected in my weakness; therefore, I most gladly boast in my infirmities that the power of Christ may rest upon me. And I still prefer grace to healing any day!

You have read about my personal struggles as I tried to understand why Bill has these medical issues. I have revealed my fears, disappointments, anger, confusion, and anxiety during these past years. I did not like the pit God had put us in when there appeared to be no medical hope back in 2006. I couldn't understand why God didn't just heal Bill when he first got cancer for I knew hundreds of people were praying for healing and continue to do so. So many feelings and questions! I don't have all the answers; I do not fully understand everything, nor do I know what the next months might hold, but I do know what God has done in my life. I'm a different person because of this journey with cancer. God has also been gracious in allowing me to see insights regarding some of those why questions. I want to share this personal letter explaining one of the whys.

Bill received this on April 10, 2008, from the wife of one of Eric Thomas's friends following the memorial service for Eric.

Dear Mr. Betts:

I needed to write you because I have an answer to a question you may have had. You see, I know you are a leukemia survivor. I am sure there was a time or two during your fight, maybe when you were tired or maybe when it felt darkest, that you asked God questions: "Why? Why me? Why am I going through this? Why cancer? I know why."

The reason is that you were the answer to my family's prayers. We never called for you by name or even knew how God would work, but we recently discovered that God indeed answered them by using you.

My husband's best friend (Eric Thomas) was diagnosed with leukemia in 2006. He had a good initial prognosis, but we were more concerned about his salvation more than his physical condition. Over the course of the next year or so, we were able to see him about five times. We limited our visits because we never wanted to put him in danger by exposing him to a family of five's germs. Early in Eric's treatment my husband spoke about Christ, but Eric didn't seem to be very receptive or open.

From the time we found out about his condition, we prayed for him. We prayed that God would find a way to soften his heart, that God would find a way to get close to him. We all prayed, we prayed every day, we prayed for his salvation.

As we sat at the funeral of Eric Thomas and you spoke to everyone about how you had led Eric to Christ and he was in heaven, our hearts were filled with joy! God had heard our prayers and answered them. The heaviness and sorrow were instantly replaced with light and hope.

Mr. Betts, God may have other purposes for allowing you to walk through the fire of leukemia, but I know that there are no coincidences in life. God timed your disease, laid out your path to Houston, and set you in front of Eric because we prayed and asked God to provide a way for Eric to find salvation.

The entire family wanted to let you know how much we appreciate your spiritual commitment that even during your own time of suffering, like the apostle Paul, you still proclaimed the glory of Christ to all.

There are no adequate words to express our gratitude for allowing God to work through you, but I hope the knowledge of how God used you will strengthen your walk.

In reading that note, there is little doubt my awesome God has done some amazing things during this journey of faith. Looking back has given me a better appreciation of how God was using every circumstance to fulfill His plans. The entire experience gave me a focus on Christ I wouldn't have gained any other way. I witnessed God's grace, power, mercy, and love. God is just and holy. He has all the power and authority to carry out His plan and purpose for He has all the armies of heaven and among the inhabitants of the earth and none can restrain Him from doing what he plans to do.

I have a God who eternally loves me and has the mighty power to direct my paths through every experience of this life and ultimately take me to heaven, all for the good of His people and all to the praise of His glorious grace and name.

CHAPTER 27

The Journey Continues

After returning to FBC Lawrenceburg, Bill preached a series of eighteen sermons on "A Portrait of Providence," using the life of Joseph to show God's faithfulness. The impact of this life story is that Joseph never knew the end from the beginning. Only God knew where Joseph's life was going because He "ordered his steps" (see Ps. 37:23) and "directed his paths" (see Prov. 3:6).

And so He does in both of our lives. In those early days of dealing with Bill's stem-cell transplant and in those quiet, uncomfortable night hours of waiting at the hospital, I reminded my heart that God is ultimately in control of Bill's life as well as mine. Psalm 119:75–77 (NKJV) says, "I know, O LORD, that Your judgments are right, and that in faithfulness You have afflicted me. Let, I pray, Your merciful kindness be for my comfort according to Your word to Your servant. Let Your tender mercies come to me, that I may live; for Your law is my delight."

Joseph may have thought numerous times that he was going to die but not if God still had plans for him. He was immortal until he had completed God's plans and purposes. Bill and I are immortal until we have completed God's plans and purposes. In one of Bill's sermons he said confidently, "I reassured myself that Christ killed death, so I have nothing to fear. In the place of death, He gave me life eternal. What an incredible exchange."

One of the greatest lessons I learned from Joseph is that it is not my place to assess opinions on what is bad and what is good. What Joseph may have thought was bad turned out to be for his good. So life-changing for Joseph was this concept that at the end of the story he told his brothers, "You meant evil against me; but God meant it for good" (Gen. 50:20 NKJV). Cancer may intend evil for my family, but God is making it work to His purposes, giving beauty for ashes and showing that "God is the strength of my heart and my portion forever" (Ps. 73:26).

No child of God is exempt from trouble, for Job 5:7 (NKJV) says, "Yet man is born to trouble, as the sparks fly upward." God never promised a perpetual rose garden free of black spots and mold. I learned that I do not need to live in a kind of cause-and-effect Christianity where every time something happens to me I immediately think, "What have I done that is causing this to happen to me?" My conscience will take me back to something that happened in the past that I have confessed and repented, and, by the grace and blood of Christ, I have been forgiven. I don't want to get caught in that trap that leads nowhere. I will never live a victorious Christian life if I continue to look back with guilt.

I learned that I did not need to let past sins appear as the cause of each problem I encounter. My sins have been cast as far as the east is from the west and God remembers them no more when I go through the process of repentance and reconciliation. The trials I face today are with few exceptions designed with sanctifying motives. Sometimes I may not have a clear understanding as to the reason for a particular problem, but I need to yield to the wise and loving Father who always does what is best because He made me, and His purpose for me is to conform me into the image of His beloved Son.

The proper response to trouble and adversities is to examine whether I have brought them on by personally violating God's biblical principles or my conscience is clear realizing God has some purposes through these trials. God will use every circumstance and situation to make me into the kind of person He wants me to be. I just need to maintain an attitude of patient endurance to understand God's plan in allowing me to experience these afflictions. The hymn "How Firm a Foundation" states, "The flames shall not hurt thee; I only design thy dross to consume and thy gold to refine." Strength and weakness of heart are found not when everything is going our way but when flames of suffering test the mettle of our character. As gold and silver are refined by fire, the human heart is revealed and developed in the presence of pain and suffering. The ultimate purpose and design are to create in me the likeness of Jesus Christ.

My greatest challenge was to allow my heart to be searched and molded as God took me through this journey with one goal in mind, to conform me to the image of His Son in new ways. There were times when things seemed to be so out of control that I felt like I was free-falling into a deep, dark pit. I would hit the bottom of that hurtful, undesirable, murky pit and cry out in great trepidation. But in those moments God showed me the light of His countenance and His all-sufficiency to intercept me and place me onto a solid foundation.

Once you get to that lowest depth in your life where there's nothing you can do, there's God. Whoever said, "God never puts on us more than we can handle," has never been to the pit. At that depth of human hopelessness,

I discovered the strength and sufficiency of Almighty God. Not until I discovered that the situation was more than I could handle and that my life was out of my control did I discover that life is securely in His control. I experienced some great lessons that can only be learned while living in a pit.

God's riches in glory are the believer's supplies. All I need is already provided awaiting my appropriation. Any lack of resources for daily trials and challenges is not due to a shortage of God's reserves but a failure to claim that which has been allocated for my daily needs. The knowledge that God has already provided all that I need and more motivates my prayers with bold assurance that He not only hears me but that will also respond in a way that restores my hope and trust.

In coping with Bill's cancer over the years, we could become absorbed with the disease. Life seems to revolve around doctors and treatment schedules, fatigue and sleepless nights. In the doldrums of this maddening malady, God began showing me that this is not about a disease of the body; this is about something spiritual and eternal. This is what the apostle Paul was talking about, "We do not lose heart. Even though our outward man is perishing, yet the inward man is being renewed day by day" (2 Cor. 4:16 NKJV). I believe so completely in the sovereign work of God that I am OK with Bill's disease. I need not lose heart. You may think this approach is a bit unusual, but it is what I believe the Scriptures teach. If my Heavenly Father designed to put Bill and me through all of this, I do not question His wisdom or His love.

Now, having accepted God's design for Bill and me and experiencing the perishing of the outward man, I realized I was completely overlooking one big aspect. Part of 2 Corinthians 4:16 says, "The inward man is being renewed day by day," and that had been off my radar screen. I had not even set up a file folder for "renewing." My approach was more stoic than spiritual. I was thinking I had to bear with my circumstances. God was thinking I should be benefiting from them. I was hoping for remission for Bill; God was working toward renewal.

God had a more extensive work to do in me than simply to heal Bill's cancer. Actually, if that's all He had done, I would be no better off than I was in 1998 when Bill was first diagnosed. The greater would not be physical but spiritual, the renewing of the inner man. God was showing me how to live. I can tell you that both Bill and I are not the same people we were in 1998 before cancer came into our world!

Through this journey God has taught me some insights that are so clearly set forth in Scripture that I generally passed over them with a "Yes, I'm doing that," "Yes, I understand that principle." One of the first lessons I learned through this journey was to learn to live where I live. I don't mean geographically. I mean that I am to live at this moment in time under the circumstances as they are. I was living for the future, out there somewhere when cancer was not going to be a part of my family's life and all of us were going to be healthy. Each day came and went with not much learning and renewing. James said, "What is your life? It is even a vapor that appears for a little time and then vanishes away" (James 4:14 NKJV). I wasn't valuing the gift of a day, let alone a moment.

Now I awaken with the thought, *This day is a gift from God who loves me so much that He is sharing it with me. He's ordered my steps, and Providence has laid out the path.* With great anticipation I begin each new day with a desire to know my Savior more deeply and intimately, fully aware that each day will have its challenges and its blessings. But as I said earlier, I will not prejudge the events of the day as bad or good, as that is not within my comprehension. Everything that happens that day works "together for good to those who love God, to those who are the called according to His purpose" (Rom. 8:28 NKJV). Joseph may not have known this verse, but he did believe that his God was watching over him and would take care of him whatever the problem.

God works for the good of those who love Him in all things, not just in the triumphs and successes but also in the dungeons. I used to think that "all things working for our good" meant that God would give me an abundance of sunshine and the absence of rain. This idea failed to help me when my life turned upside down living in a pit that appeared to have no way out. What I learned is that the "good" of those who love Him is ultimately my conformity to Jesus Christ.

Accepting the things that I have no power to change as a part of God's design was another lesson I learned along this journey. There were times when Joseph's life and mine came together. I was being carried along by a force much stronger than me, and I could not see where it was leading. Feeling trapped was an emotion I experienced often. Like a fish caught on the hook, I was being pulled along. At times I resisted; at times I fought it. I did everything I could to get loose, yet I could not. I came to understand that some matters absolutely cannot be changed. This concept freed me of much frustration and anxiety over those things that were not going to change.

The light actually came on the brightest when I discovered that unchangeable circumstances were by God's design to show me my weakness and His attributes. The unchangeable made me cry out to my sovereign God for help. Now this is an area that He loves to hear from His children. He loves it when we show our need for Him. And most of the times He's not going to change a thing. He's going to let us discover how much more of Himself is revealed through those things that are the unchangeable and unmovable.

My biggest concern is that I not forget that God is overseeing my life just as He was before Bill had cancer. "There are many plans in a man's heart, nevertheless the Lord's counsel—that will stand" (Prov. 19:21 NKJV). Two biblical truths must always be kept in perspective while going through any adversity. First, God's plan is to mature us in the faith. "But grow in the grace and knowledge of our Lord and Savior Jesus Christ" (2 Pet. 3:18). There is purpose in God's design for me when I am in those unchangeable circumstances. I need to look for the character qualities God wants to build in my life as well as those character flaws He wants to remove.

The second truth is to recognize that trials reveal our needs and God's sufficiency. If we never had trials and adversities, we would never know the grace and power of God to resolve them for His glory and our good. Whenever I find myself in a predicament and I begin to feel desperation and lack of trust, I know that God has put me there so that I might face my weakness and find the power of the Holy Spirit able to produce the fruit of the Spirit in my heart.

Over these years I have experienced deeper insights into God's nature and ways while witnessing Bill's battle with cancer than I ever did when he was healthy. God's faithfulness has shined the brightest during those many dark nights when I saw Bill so sick. I felt so helpless. Then in the moment of my despair, God would draw near me and reassure me that He was in complete control. His grace is sufficient; His strength is made complete in my weakness. Bill still has chronic lymphocytic leukemia and now with the diagnosis of melanoma the treatments for remission become more complex with fewer options, and yet Bill and I have found peace, strength, and hope that enable us in everything to "give thanks; for this is the will of God in Christ Jesus concerning us"

God has given me this incredible peace, and hope floods my soul and calms my heart. His peace is a tranquility that sustains me. All of the fervent and faithful prayers have been a major source of strength and encouragement for both Bill and I. I look at Bill and I'm amazed, and thankful that Bill feels good most of the time. In fact Bill's doctor told one of the other oncologist that Bill is one of his sickest patients, but is healthier looking than any of his other patients. We can only credit God for His sustaining grace and renewing of strength daily. Bill's body may not have completely beaten cancer, but God has enlarged my outlook of what it means to beat cancer—real victory, triumph over cancer in my mind and spirit. I have found God's love and power to be all sufficient, and that's real victory.

As Bill's wife, I would much prefer that my husband did not have to suffer or to go through these dreadful diseases, including all the setbacks and disappointments that now appeared to have become unavoidable, inevitable, and inescapable; but I know that these ordeals are a part of God's plan. He does not always take away our problems. Instead He gives the grace to live with them. God knows each turn in our horizon. I never want to forget that God loves me, and He loves to do the improbable and specializes in the impossible. He can move even the mountains if He desires. He is far too big to be in a box, for nothing is bigger or more powerful than my Heavenly Father, including conquering cancer. He is a God of miracles. I have seen some of those miracles. I asked Bill this question several months after we returned home from Houston, "Would you go through all these adversities again?" Bill said, "Yes, I would because out of these, God has been glorified." I agree with my husband. God has done a marvelous work in our lives, and that's just one of those miracles He has allowed me to see. He has many more to do! I know God will continue to transform this cancer ordeal into many wonderful blessings as Bill and I move toward our predetermined destination for we are made by God and for God.

I don't know how many more years Bill will live with his cancer. He might make it to sixty-five; or if he has inherited his father's longevity, he may just reach the age of one hundred. Bill's dad celebrated that century milestone in March 2009. But regardless how long Bill or I live on this earth, one day all of our hearts will stop. That will be the end of our bodies here on earth, but it won't be the end of us, for we have put our faith and trust in Jesus Christ. Our lives will just be beginning. Bill and I will be with God in heaven forever and we pray we can say, "We fought the good fight, we have finished the race, and have kept the faith."

In the meantime, Bill and I will live each day as if it is the last day we have here on earth. We do not linger on those "why" questions but focus on all that God is doing in our lives as a result of cancer. We do not lose hope, for we are going to invest our energies in walking by faith no matter what comes our way, knowing that Jesus Christ is able to do immeasurably more than all we ask or imagine, according to His power that is at work within us. Bill and I see God's providential hand in our lives and we know that moving forward means facing the future with the Lord, having a hope for today and especially a hope for the tomorrows. Life may continue to be difficult, maybe even painful, and for now it is imperfect. But still it is good, for in all these things nothing can separate us from God's lavish expressions of love. God's grace is immeasurable, His mercy inexhaustible, and His peace inexpressible.

"Now to Him who is able to keep you from stumbling, and to make you stand in the presence of His glory blameless with great joy, to the only God our Savior, through Jesus Christ our Lord, be glory, majesty, dominion and authority, before all time and now and forever. Amen." Jude 24 & 25

Questions and Thoughts to Ponder:

Week 1

1. For what purposes would God use your adversities?

2. What would be the proper response to trouble and afflictions for a Christian?

3. When it is unclear as to the reason for a particular problem, what should be the response?

4. What do you need to do to discover His purposes?

5. Do you think God has something else in mind for you than your earthly goals?

6. Have you ever felt trapped in an unchangeable situation? What was it?

7. There is purpose in God's design for you when you are in those unchangeable circumstances. Look for character qualities God wants to build within you and for character flaws He wants to remove. What are some of those character qualities and flaws?

Week 2

1. Why is patience so important in understanding adversity?

2. Do you think God's people are exempt from trials?

3. Put in your own words what Romans 8:28, means to you.

4. Do you think that "all things working for our good" means that God will give us an abundance of sunshine and the absence of rain? What happens when you find yourself facing an adversity?

5. No child of God is exempt from trouble. The truth is, this earthly life will have many ups and downs, but there is only one way a person can obtain a life of "Happily Ever-After". Where and how does one find that life and who can provide it for you?

6. Some people are still living with a form of cause-and-effect Christianity believing that every time something happens to them they stop and think, "What is it we did that caused this to happen to us?" Can a Christian live a victorious life lf they continue to look back with quilt?

7. As you accept your lack of control over your life, you find you do have control over your choices. What are some of your choices?

Week 3

1. What God is doing in your life is not because you have merited His favor. You understand you cannot earn salvation, which is a gift of God's free grace. But that's true not only of your coming to Christ, but also of your living for Christ. Does God not repay you for the good things you've done by making good things happen to you? If that were the basis of God's dealing with you, how can you explain when bad things happen in your life? What God does in your life is it motivated by what you do?

2. Why is it so hard to accept the unchangeable as a part of God's design? Do you have control of your choices? And what choices do you have?

3. Do the friction and the discord spring from your very humanness?

4. Part of learning to count your blessings is accepting that many of them you would not have chosen if it had been left to you. Why must you give up any attempt to compare what was with what might have been?

5. How can you accept the path God has set you upon and the blessings from whatever circumstance of life may bring to you?

6. Why is it hard to accept God's will when it comes to those we love?

Week 4

1. The apostle Paul declared there was something he bore, perhaps an illness, an adversity. We don't know exactly what it was. It was only with God's presence that Paul could bear his burden. Are your thorns in the flesh really a gift that forces you to turn to God?

2. Can God take an adversity that will stir you mind and heart turning it into what will keep you closest to Him?

3. Do you think God uses every circumstance and situation to make you into the kind of people He wants you to be?

4. When you are in the pits of the problem and the throws of the trial, what promises do you run to? What promises give you hope and comfort?

5. How does one get through the trials and difficulties of life?

6. Do you believe that God has an ultimate design that He has planned for you and that the many roads God takes you down are His unfolding plan and design for you?

7. What are your thoughts about chance or luck?

Week 5

1. God didn't just put you here on earth to fulfill a "to-to list". Is He more interested in what you are than what you do?

2. Every material possession that you place so much importance upon here on earth will wear away and disappear, yet why is it that you cling to it and you seek to increase your possessions? Why is it that you hungry for more, just this one thing more, first I will have that, then I will be content, then I will be happy?

3. Do you think that sometimes the greatest challenge to finding the right answers to the whys....is learning to ask the correct questions? Do you feel the greatest moments of your life have been masked by impossible questions?

4. Do you ever feel like you don't know what to do? What do you do then?

5. There is no question everyone will have storms in their lives. The challenge is not how to avoid them, for they will come. But how will you use those storms? What will you learn from them? What lessons will you take from those encounters?

6. Do you think bitterness and hope are choices not circumstances?

7. Is bitterness the result of doing things my way? And Is Hope the result of doing things God's way?

8. Does a proper view of God determine my attitude?

Week 6

1. One day my heart will stop, and that will be the end of my body --- but is that the end of you?

2. There are things in life in which you find yourself totally helpless to do anything about them. Does God's plan have lessons that cannot be learned anywhere else except in the situation you find yourself facing?

3. Can even the heartache of a death of a love one be transformed into something good?

4. Do you believe that your journey here on earth is orchestrated by the sovereign God of Heaven as was the creation of the entire world?

5. Are you the object of God's sovereign care?

6. Do you believe that what God is doing in your life is not finished yet until He calls you home?

7. You can focus on your problems, or you can focus on God's purposes. God may not heal your love one and take away all your problems, but you can focus on God and others. God has promised to strengthen your character, give you a ministry of helping other people, and He will give you a testimony while He continues to draw you closer to Him.

8. Sometimes you must yield to the always wise and loving Father who made you for Himself and maintains a single purpose for you – to conform you into the image of His beloved Son.

9. Recognize that trials reveal your needs and God's sufficiency. Whenever you find yourself in a predicament and you begin to feel those feelings of impatience, selfishness, ungratefulness, quick temper, or lack of trust, know that God has put you there that you might face your weakness and find the power of the Holy Spirit able to produce the fruit of the Spirit in your heart.

10. Salvation is by grace through faith in Jesus Christ alone. Christ died for our sins, was buried, and rose again for our justification, declaring us righteous before God. The Gospel of Christ is the power of God to salvation for everyone who believes. The God who created the universe is the God you can know. For whoever calls upon the name of the Lord Jesus Christ will be saved and will live with God for eternity.

LaVergne, TN USA
24 February 2010
174165LV00003B/2/P